The Ghost Train

A PLAY IN THREE ACTS

BY

ARNOLD RIDLEY

SAMUEL FRENCH, INC.

25 WEST 45TH STREET, NEW YORK, N. Y.

811 WEST 7TH STREET, LOS ANGELES, CALIF.

SAMUEL FRENCH, LTD.

26 SOUTHAMPTON STREET, STRAND, W.C.2, LONDON

"THE GHOST TRAIN"

ALL RIGHTS RESERVED

The Ghost Train

ACT ONE

SCENE: *The Waiting Room of the Railway Station at Clear Vale Junction.*

It is a dingy square room with a low sloping ceiling. The walls are of a dirty, grimy plaster, very much smoked up, and the woodwork is a very dirty, dingy dark brown, much scarred with use. The Right Upper corner of the room has been partitioned off with a board partition, not reaching to the ceiling, behind which is the ticket office off R. There is a ticket window down R. in this partition, with a shutter which slides up and down, and above it is the inscription, "TICKETS." Up R. above this window is a door leading off R. into the office, above which is the inscription, "STATION MASTER." The entire back wall is taken up with a door at C. opening into the room, which is one step up and leads out onto the platform; also a wide low window on either side of the door, each one consisting of two wide sashes of four lights each, hinged at the sides, and opening like casement windows. The glass in these windows is so thickly coated with dirt as to make it impossible to distinguish anything through them. At the Left stands a round railway station stove with pipe leading into the wall, the glow of the fire seen when the stove is opened.

7

Suspended from the ceiling, C., *is an old-fashioned Rochester oil lamp which has been wired up for electricity, and over the ticket window at* R. *and below the stove on the wall at* L. *are two plain old single light electric brackets, each with an old round tin shade on it. On the walls are, at* R. *below the ticket window, a rack filled with dog-eared Maine timetables of various railways; up* R., *in the corner behind the ticket office door, is a narrow blackboard on which is chalked up some few arrival and departure times of trains, and on either side of this blackboard is a peg driven into the hall to hang coats on. At Left of the door up* C., *between it and the window, is a large calendar with the date torn to Friday 13th, and just below it is another small rack containing time-tables. On the back wall at the Left of the window* L. *is a large soiled, dingy framed steamship lithograph, and on the wall* L. *are two soiled framed railway maps, one up stage and one down. Driven into the wall between these maps, and directly back of the stove, are two more pegs for hanging coats. Through the open window of the ticket office at* R. *can be seen a large advertising calendar, and through the open door of the office is seen a large pigeonhole ticket rack, filled with tickets. There is also seen through this door an oaken office swivel chair with an old cushion on its seat. The floor of the room is of plain boards, the ground cloth being painted to show this. The furnishings of the room consist of a plain, straight old armchair away down at* R., *a rather high wooden stand on which is an old crockery water-cooler, with an old enamel-ware cup hanging by a chain, which stands in the niche at* R. *between the ticket office window and door, a waiting room bench with back to it which stands against the back wall up* R.C. *An old trunk, tied with rope and with shipping labels on, which is against* L. *wall. A plain old wooden straight chair which is up* L. *near the stove. Another waiting-room bench with back which stands against the wall down* L., *an old square of zinc under the stove at* L.; *an old battered coalhod in which is a small fire-shovel and a poker stands back of the stove on zinc. Down at* C., *standing across the stage, is a battered, heavy old table, six feet long, and at* C. *in front of it is an old battered four-foot bench, without back.*

TIME: *Ten-thirty at night, in early spring.*

AT RISE: *The room is dimly lighted by the light from the Center hanging lamp and the two side brackets. The door and window of the ticket office at* R. *are both open, and a dim light shows out. A faint red glow of a dying fire comes through the openings of the closed door of the stove. The door up* C. *is closed.*

As the door C. *is opened there is seen to be almost complete blackness outside. The CLANG-CLANG-CLANG of a crossing signal bell is heard before the Curtain rises, and as the Curtain goes up is heard the sound of a distant train WHISTLE, followed by the increasing ROAR of the approaching train, which grows louder and louder until it dashes into the station, with the loud noise of the ENGINE, the GRINDING of the brakes, and the HISSING of the escaping steam. As the WHISTLE of the train is first heard in the distance,* SAUL *is seen to look out of the ticket window, then put on his cap, take a lighted railroad lantern, and come from the office* R., *crossing quickly to door up* c. *and exits, closing door after him. A TELEGRAPH instrument is heard busily clicking in the ticket office off* R. *As the train comes to a stop in the station, the SMOKE from the engine comes drifting in through the cracks around the door and windows up back. There is heard the puffing of the ENGINE and the measured ringing of the bell, while the train is in the station, also the VOICES of the train-men, and the BUMPING of trunks and milk-cans being unloaded. At the same time the VOICES of the angry* PASSENGERS *in altercation with* SAUL *are heard. After a moment of this the* CONDUCTOR *is heard to shout, "All aboard! All aboard!" There is a loud HISS of the steam, a long blast of the WHISTLE just outside the windows, followed by the labored PUFFS of the engine in starting, and the RUMBLE of the starting train. The LIGHTS from the coaches flash past the windows as the train gathers speed, and as the ROAR DIMINISHES, and with a FAINT BLAST of the whistle, dies away in the distance. As the sound of the train is dying away, the door* c. *opens and* ELSIE WINTHROP *and* RICHARD WINTHROP *enter, both carrying bags. They have been quarreling, and are both in a bad temper.*

ELSIE. *(Entering* c.; *crossing* L. *to stove)* I suppose this is the waiting-room!

RICHARD. *(Entering after her, closes door and drops bag up* L.C.*)* I suppose so. It looks like it. *(Crossing down* c.*)*

ELSIE. The stove's out—or pretty nearly. Just the kind of a cheerful place you would bring me to! *(Crossing and angrily putting her bag on table* c.*)*

RICHARD. *(Crossing front to* R.C.*)* Bring you——
That's a laugh.

ELSIE. *(Coming* C.*)* It's damp, dirty and disagreeable.

RICHARD. It's disagreeable, right enough.

ELSIE. And a lot you care!

RICHARD. Maybe I'm used to it.

ELSIE. Thanks!

RICHARD. *(Crossing* C. *to her)* Well, for Heaven's sake—is it my fault? I'm not the Managing Director of the darn Company. How could I help the wretched engine stalling, for no reason at all?

ELSIE. We should have gone by car, as I wanted to in the first place.

RICHARD. *(Turning away* R.C.*)* Oh, you're always right! And that young idiot in the train, with the feather in his hat, seemed quite amused when I told him we'd missed the connection.

ELSIE. *(Turning up* C.*)* And you swore at him!

RICHARD. Well—why shouldn't I? *(Turning up* R.*)* Here, let's find out what there is in here. *(Exits up* R. *into ticket office.* ELSIE *stamps her foot angrily, and exits after him.)*

SAUL. *(Enters up* C., *speaking as he comes in)* Well, this here is the only place! *(He steps to* R. *of door as he enters, and is followed by* CHARLES MURDOCK, *carrying two bags, and* PEGGY MURDOCK, *carrying one bag.* STOP TELEGRAPH.*)*

CHARLES. *(Looking about the room)* Good Lord —what a hole!

PEGGY. *(Following him in)* Oh, Charlie! *(*CHARLES *puts his two bags down* L.C. *under window, leaving his hat on top of them.* PEGGY *places her bag on table* C.*)*

SAUL. *(Up* C. *by door, speaking off* C.*)* Hey— you! What are you doing? Not that way—— *(Exits* C. *as he speaks, closing door.)*

CHARLES. *(Crossing down across front to* R.C.,

taking in room) Well—this looks a nice cheerful little dump, I must say.

PEGGY. *(Following to* R.C. *over to him)* Never mind, dear.

CHARLES. But I do mind! And, in case we forget, this is our wedding night.

PEGGY. *(Dreamily)* Yes!

CHARLES. We don't want to hang about here long. And what will they say at the hotel if we don't turn up?

PEGGY. *(Laughingly)* I hope they won't think you changed your mind at the last minute.

CHARLES. What a joke! *(Crossing over to* L.C.*)* Tonight, of all nights, to be stuck in a place like this! *(Turning at* L.C. *and indicating room)* Look at it! No—this is no joke! I'm hungry, and you're tired, and we both want to get to our hotel. It was tough missing the train! *(Turning away to* L.*)*

PEGGY. *(Coming to him* L.*)* That was Mother's fault. I knew we would be late.

CHARLES. I'm furious! When we've only got this one week, before I have to leave you and go abroad, I begrudge every moment wasted.

PEGGY. *(*L. *by him, putting her arms about his neck)* Let's forget about that, dear. Let's pretend we shall be together always.

CHARLES. *(Putting his arms around her)* I'm sorry, old girl. I won't gloom, tonight of all nights. There's one thing about it, though—all those other folks seem to have cleared off, and we're alone together. Give me a kiss, and I'll smile again.

PEGGY. *(Snuggling closer into his embrace)* Darling!

CHARLES. *(Embracing her)* Darling! *(They kiss. As they do so the door* C. *opens and* MISS BOURNE *enters, followed by* SAUL.*)*

MISS BOURNE. *(Carrying a covered parrot cage and an armfull of cushions and rugs; sees* CHARLES *and* PEGGY *and speaks as she comes through the door)* Oh—love birds! (CHARLES *and* PEGGY *start apart in confusion, and he crosses front to* R.C., *where he meets* MISS BOURNE, *who crosses down to him.* PEGGY *remains down* L.) I say—this is the waiting-room, I presume? Well, there's not much waiting about you, is there? *(Giving him a slight push. Puts rugs and cushions on table* C.*)* Don't mind me. Get on with it! Get on with it! *(Crossing over to stove* L.*)* Oh, what a bright and cheery fire! I shall be done on this side, if I stop here long. *(Crosses to bench* C. *and sits, placing cage on floor beside her)* And what a smoke!

CHARLES. They do say that where there's smoke there's fire—but not in this case.

SAUL. *(Who has closed door up* C., *crossing to stove)* I'm sure it's a lovely fire, for this time of night.

(ELSIE *and* RICHARD *enter up* R., RICHARD *going to up* R.C.)

PEGGY. *(At* L., *crossing a little to* C.*)* We shall have to put up with it until the next train.

SAUL. *(*L.C.*)* I keep on telling her, there ain't no "next train."

CHARLES. *(*R.C.*)* What?

SAUL. There ain't no more trains till seven tomorrow mornin'.

CHARLES. *(Crossing front to* SAUL*)* But I say— I've got to get this young lady—er—my wife to Rockland tonight.

SAUL. Well, you ain't a-goin' to do it.

CHARLES. We must order a special.

SAUL. "Special"! From here? There ain't no such thing on this line. (ELSIE *crosses down* R. *and sits.)*

CHARLES. Where can we hire a car?

SAUL. Nowhere—that I knows of.

CHARLES. Well, what can we do?

SAUL. I don't know what you'll do. I know what I'm going to do. I'm goin' home. *(Crosses up* C.*)*

CHARLES. *(*L.C.*)* Oh, Hell!

PEGGY. Oh!

CHARLES. I'm sorry, Pegs, but it looks as if we're in something of a mess.

PEGGY. It can't be helped, and I don't mind. *(Crosses down* L.*)*

CHARLES. But Good Lord—this is terrible.

RICHARD. *(Up* R.C.*)* Look here—let me talk to this fellow. Now, see here, Porter—— *(Crossing to* SAUL.*)*

SAUL. Excuse me, sir—Station Master!

RICHARD. Well, then, "Station Master"—do you really mean to say we can't get any further tonight?

SAUL. Not on this line—you can't.

RICHARD. Well, where's the nearest hotel?

SAUL. *Rockland!*

CHARLES. Oh, good Lord!

RICHARD. But there must be some place or other where we can stay for the night?

SAUL. There's a farm down the road.

RICHARD. Don't you live anywhere?

SAUL. Yes.

RICHARD. Where?

SAUL. Rockland.

RICHARD. Well, how do you get there?

SAUL. Motorcycle.

RICHARD. *(Crossing a little down* R.C.*)* Well, ladies and gentlemen—it looks as if we shall have to stay here until morning.

CHARLES. *(A little up* L.C.*)* I say, where's that fellow with the feather in his hat that was so amused when the engine stalled?

RICHARD. That idiot!

SAUL. There's another gentleman out on the platform.

CHARLES. I wonder if he still thinks it's funny?

RICHARD. If he finds anything to laugh at in this hole, I'll murder him—him and his damned hat!

MISS BOURNE. *(Seated on bench down C.)* Well, why wasn't he summoned or something—and why couldn't he leave the emergency cord alone?

(TEDDIE DEAKIN's VOICE is heard calling off C.)

TEDDIE. *(Calling outside up C.)* Oh, Porter— Porter! I say, Station Master!

SAUL. *(Opening door up C.)* Yes, sir.

TEDDIE. *(Entering in door up C., laden down with golf-bag, large kit-bag, rug, bundle of newspapers, rubber air cushion, and a vacuum bottle)* I say— where can I get a taxi around here?

SAUL. *(Up by C. door)* Taxi? There ain't no such thing anywhere around these parts.

EDDIE. *(Coming a little down C. into the room)* That's too bad! Do you know, a silly ass out there called me a silly ass, out there.

SAUL. Why, there ain't nobody out there, sir.

TEDDIE. I know. That's what annoyed me. I say —do you know, all this reminds me very much of a night I spent in a Golf Clubhouse, outside Harrowgate—— No, it was Matlock—— Anyway, it was one of those places where they have sulphur water. I remember that, because we were all so frightfully depressed at the time, and it was raining—you know rain, don't you—and there was a man there, and he—— *(Noticing that the OTHERS are all annoyed)* I say, you don't seem to be very much interested, do you?

RICHARD. *(Turning away down R.)* Frankly—I must confess that we're not.

TEDDIE. *(Crossing down R.C. by table, and puts*

his papers, cushion, bottle and rug down) Oh, that's too bad. I say—what a topping little crib! Well, here we all are, then—and what were you priceless old things discussing?

RICHARD. *(Down* R.*)* Nothing important—and we were all unanimous on the subject.

TEDDIE. *(Putting his golf-bag in corner up* R., *takes off his coat and drops it on bench up* R.*)* Good egg! So we're here till morning, what? *(Comes back down* R.C.*)*

CHARLES. *(Down* L.*)* Yes.

TEDDIE. It's rather priceless, don't you think—a little adventure—something to relieve the bally monotony—what?

CHARLES. It may be an adventure for you, but we're in the devil of a mess.

TEDDIE. That's too bad! Now, I'm quite enjoying myself.

MISS BOURNE. *(Seated on bench* C.*)* I say, young man—have you no sense of responsibility?

TEDDIE. Responsibility? Whatever's that?

MISS BOURNE. Your ignorance of the word hardly surprises me.

TEDDIE. Oh, come, now, you're not peeved with me?

MISS BOURNE. Your lack of concern is monstrous, considering that you are the direct cause of this unpleasant situation.

TEDDIE. *(Down* R.C. *by end of table)* But my good woman!

MISS BOURNE. *(Seated bench* C., *angrily)* I am not a good woman—— No—no—no—I don't mean that. I mean that I will not be addressed with unwarranted familiarity.

TEDDIE. But I say, you must be fair, you know. How could I help my hat blowing away?

RICHARD. *(Down* R.*)* Well, if you stick your head out of the window. that's apt to happen.

TEDDIE. *(Turning to him)* But I say, old thing, I was only watching the sparks from the engine. I love sparks. I once wrote a little poem about them.
"If sparks were larks, and sang at night,
'Twould make my evenings oh, so bright
If sparks were larks."

RICHARD. Losing your beastly hat was no excuse for pulling the emergency-cord.

TEDDIE. Don't you think so?

RICHARD. No!!

TEDDIE. Well, I do. It was a jolly nice hat. I only bought it last week. Besides, I've always wanted to pull the communication cord. It's such a refreshing idea, don't you think so?

RICHARD. Damn it, man—haven't you any sense of decency?

TEDDIE. Decency? What do you mean?

RICHARD. You don't seem to realize the facts of the case.

TEDDIE. I hate facts.

RICHARD. Then giving you some will give me great pleasure. First of all, you stick your fool head out of the window, like the silly ass that you are——

TEDDIE. Yes.

RICHARD. Yes, and then when your beastly hat blows off, you pull the emergency cord, and stop the train on an incline——

TEDDIE. Yes—yes.

RICHARD. Yes, and consequently we miss our train connection, and have to spend the night in this God-forsaken hole——

TEDDIE. Yes, that's quite right.

RICHARD. And now, instead of being sorry—why, damn it all, sir—you strut around as if you'd done us all a favor.

TEDDIE. I say—you don't seem quite to like me, do you?

RICHARD. If I were to tell you my candid opinion——

ELSIE. *(Seated down* R.*)* Oh, don't haggle, Richard. Surely things are bad enough without a quarrel. Here we are—and here we've got to stop!

TEDDIE. *(*R.C.*)* Rightiho! And I'm going to pick out a nice soft spot. *(Crosses and sits on bench up* R.*)*

SAUL. *(Up* C.; *coming a little down)* Beg pardon, ladies—but you can't stop here.

ELSIE. *(Rising)* What! ⎫
RICHARD. Eh! ⎭ *(Together)*

SAUL. I said as how you can't stop here.

RICHARD. What the blazes do you mean?

SAUL. There ain't no traffic on this line at night, so we shuts everything up—signal-boxes—station—and the whole shebang! I'm off home.

RICHARD. Well, goodnight.

SAUL. Yes—but before I go, I got to lock everything up.

RICHARD. Well, this time you can't "lock everything up."

SAUL. Beg your pardon, sir—but them's my orders, and I got to obey 'em.

RICHARD. *(Angrily)* Don't be so damned idiotic. How about us?

SAUL. You ain't no concern of mine. Orders is orders. You might go to the farm.

CHARLES. *(Down* L. *Crossing little up* L.C.*)* How far is that?

SAUL. 'Bout five miles.

RICHARD. Do you expect these ladies to walk five miles, on a night like this?

SAUL. I don't expect nothin'. All I expect to do is lock up.

RICHARD. *(Angrily)* Is that so!

SAUL. You can't stop me.

CHARLES. Who's to prevent us?

SAUL. Me!

CHARLES. And are you going to throw us out?

SAUL. Yes. Mind ye, I shall be sorry to have to do it.

RICHARD. *(Taking off his hat and coat and throwing them on chair down R.)* Oh, don't you worry about that. Just make a start on me. *(Starts toward* SAUL, *who draws back up* C.*)*

SAUL. Now, you keep your hands off of me. *(They ad lib. a little argument together.)*

TEDDIE. *(Rising)* I say, this is perfectly priceless. *(Crossing down between* RICHARD *and* SAUL *up* R.C., *turning as he does so, and backing down around to down* C.*)* Seconds out of the ring! Round one! Ting-a-ling! *(Starts to sit on bench* C. *and almost sits on* MISS BOURNE's *lap.)*

MISS BOURNE. *(Pushing him off. He sits beside her)* Ting-a-ling! And don't sit on me!

RICHARD. *(Up* R.C. *to* SAUL. PEGGY *crosses up* C. *to* CHARLES*)* Well—I'm waiting!

SAUL. Now, look here—— Don't you lay your hands on me.

RICHARD. I'm not going to. You were going to throw us out.

CHARLES. *(Up* L.*)* Come on, now. We're going to stay. We'll see that you don't get into any trouble. *(Taking a bill from his pocket and slipping it into* SAUL's *hand.)*

SAUL. *(As he pockets the bill)* Well—in a case like that——

CHARLES. Then it's all right, eh?

SAUL. Well, I dunno as it is—but I ain't got no choice.

*(*TEDDIE *has been annoying* MISS BOURNE *down* C. *by looking over her shoulder at the paper she is reading, and when she draws it away from him, reaching around her and trying to get it*

from the other side. He finally takes his air cushion and begins to blow it up, letting the valve leak a few times so that the air escapes into MISS BOURNE'S *ear.)*

CHARLES. That's the talk! Now, how about seeing if we can fix the place up, so the ladies will be a bit more comfortable? To begin with—this stove— *(Turning a little down toward stove.)*

SAUL. *(Up c.)* Well, now there's another fire in the ticket office. I dunno as it's any better, but you can come in and see. *(Exits R.)*

CHARLES. *(Up L. with PEGGY)* Shall we go and see, Pegs? *(He and PEGGY exit up R.)*

MISS BOURNE. *(Screws her handkerchief into her ear to escape the air from the cushion, then rises and glares at TEDDIE)* Things like you are found in cheese. *(Crosses toward door up R., leaving cage on floor by bench. TEDDIE picks it up and begins to poke inside it. She turns at door R.)* Only better looking! *(Looks up R. for cage, sees TEDDIE has it, then crosses back down c., snatches it from him, and gives his face a push, then exits up R.)*

TEDDIE. *(Rising down c.)* Oh, what a pleasant person! I'll get her telephone number. *(Crosses and exits up R.)*

RICHARD. *(Up R.C. to ELSIE, who is down R.)* Well, what do you think of this? *(SAUL closes ticket window R. from inside.)*

ELSIE. *(Crossing L., putting RICHARD's hat and coat on table c. as she passes)* Not much! You should be in your element, though!

RICHARD. *(Coming a little down R.)* I don't get you.

ELSIE. *(By stove)* Doesn't it give you a marvelous chance to domineer everyone? Already you've threatened to fight the old Station Master—and been very rude to someone half your size. A great evening for you!

RICHARD. *(Crossing to* L.C. *by her)* See here, Elsie—must we keep this up? Can't we forget it all?

ELSIE. I can't forget what you said to me this morning, if that's what you mean.

RICHARD. I admit I lost my temper this morning—but you must realize how worried I am just now. My Works Manager dying suddenly like that —yes, and Perkinson was more than that. He was an expert—clear—level-headed. A man like that isn't easy to replace.

ELSIE. And because of that, I had to suffer!

RICHARD. You must admit you were exasperating.

ELSIE. Of course—it was my fault you behaved like a pig. I might have known that.

RICHARD. I didn't say so.

ELSIE. But you meant it.

RICHARD. See here, Elsie—we've only been married a year. It seems too bad to go on like this. Let's start afresh?

ELSIE. I'm sorry, but it's too late. We must keep to our agreement.

RICHARD. But, my dear girl——

ELSIE. It's no use going all over it again. We don't hit it, and never shall.

RICHARD. Still, it seems a pity!

ELSIE. Did you suggest a separation, or did I?

RICHARD. Oh, I did, but——

ELSIE. Very well, then!

RICHARD. I was in a temper at the time—we were both in a temper.

ELSIE. I beg your pardon—*I* never lose my temper.

RICHARD. You never flare up, but——

ELSIE. What?

RICHARD. Elsie—be reasonable!

ELSIE. Oh, I'm not blaming you—you can't help it. (RICHARD *turns away to* C. *and then back again as she continues*) The truth of the matter is that we're absolutely unsuited to each other. If you'd married a timid little mouse of a girl, it would have been fine—in return for your protection and shielding arm she would have looked on you as a God, and put up with your domineering. I'm different—I don't need protection, and I won't be domineered. Your manly strength is no attraction to me, because *I* can look after myself. I've never been afraid of anything in my life.

RICHARD. (*A little up* L.C.) That's just it, Elsie —you're so damned self-reliant.

ELSIE. There you go—you're off again! I've had enough scenes for one day. I'm going into the other room. (*Starts to cross toward up* R.)

RICHARD. (*Taking a step down in front of her at* C.) Elsie—for the last time, let's start again?

ELSIE. No, Dick—I've made up my mind. (*He inclines his head and steps back out of her way. She crosses to door up* R. *and just as she reaches it, it opens quickly and* CHARLES *enters, bumping into her at door.*)

CHARLES. (*Stepping aside at door up* R.) I beg your pardon.

ELSIE. (*Very sweetly, turning in door*) Don't mention it. It's quite all right. (*She exits up* R. RICHARD *crosses and sits on bench down* C.)

CHARLES. (*Leaving door open, crosses to bench* C.) Cheerful, isn't it? (*Sits on bench* C., *beside* RICHARD.)

RICHARD. Perfectly rotten!

CHARLES. There's nothing we can do.

RICHARD. Not a thing. We shall have to put up with it until morning.

CHARLES. It's pretty bad for you, of course— but I'm in a hell of a mess.

RICHARD. We all are.

CHARLES. I—I expect you've been married some time?

RICHARD. Yes.

CHARLES. That makes it a whole lot easier.

RICHARD. Does it?

CHARLES. You see—we—my wife and I—well, we—we haven't been married very long—— *(Embarrassed, he pulls his handkerchief from his upper pocket and a shower of rice and confetti falls on the floor.)*

RICHARD. *(With a laugh, as he sees the rice)* That's all right.

CHARLES. I'm afraid that rather gives us away. Well, hang it, there's nothing to be ashamed of. We were only married this morning. But, for God's sake, don't tell the others.

RICHARD. Of course not.

CHARLES. It's wonderful to be married—to have someone to stand by you through thick and thin.

RICHARD. You've found that out?

CHARLES. You bet I have—and I'm glad I learned it soon, because we haven't much time.

RICHARD. I thought you said you'd just got married?

CHARLES. Yes—but——

RICHARD. Have *you* had a row?

CHARLES. Good Lord—no.

RICHARD. Of course not—I beg your pardon.

CHARLES. That's all right. I suppose people *do* have rows, sometimes.

RICHARD. Yes! Sometimes!

CHARLES. I can't understand it! As a matter of fact, my trouble is—my name is Murdock.

RICHARD. Murdock! Any relation to Murdock & Son?

CHARLES. Yes—I'm the son—worse luck!

RICHARD. I see.

CHARLES. Our smash is pretty well known.

RICHARD. I happened to notice it because I happen to be in the same line of business.

CHARLES. You are—— That's strange!

RICHARD. Weren't you in charge of the Canadian branch of your firm?

CHARLES. Yes, you see I was educated in England, and so I mixed in rather well with the Toronto and Montreal branch. I just had the business where I could have handled it from Boston, when the big smash came.

RICHARD. I say, what rotten luck!

CHARLES. Well, you've one competitor less, anyway. I'm clearing out—going to try my luck in South America.

RICHARD. Alone?

CHARLES. Yes—it's impossible to take the wife there. Just this little honeymoon together, and then—— Oh, it's hell!

RICHARD. *(Rising to* L.C.*)* So *you* don't want to separate?

CHARLES. *(Rising to him* C.*)* Want to separate? What a question!

RICHARD. Of course you don't—I didn't mean that.

PEGGY. *(Calling off up* R. *and entering as she speaks)* Oh, Charlie—Charlie! Where are you, Charlie?

CHARLES. *(Turns and meets her* R.C.*)* Here I am. Well, did you manage to get a wash?

PEGGY. Yes—old Methuselah managed to dig up a piece of soap and a towel, after all.

CHARLES. *(With* PEGGY *at* R.C.*)* Good! I've just been having a talk with Mr.—— *(Turning inquiringly to* RICHARD.*)*

RICHARD. *(*L.C.*)* Winthrop is my name.

CHARLES. *(Introducing them)* Peggy—meet Mr. Winthrop. Mr. Winthrop, allow me to introduce my wife, Miss Peggy—er—my wife! (PEGGY *crosses to* RICHARD. *They shake hands.*)

RICHARD. How do you do?

CHARLES. We've just discovered that we're both in the same line of business. Quite a coincidence.

RICHARD. Yes, it's very strange. *(Crosses up back of table toward* R.)

PEGGY. *(Turning around to* L. *end of table, facing him)* Oh, please don't let me drive you away.

RICHARD. Not at all. There's something I want to say to my wife. *(Exits up* R., *closing door.)*

CHARLES. *(Sits on bench at* C. *and draws* PEGGY *down at* L.C. *beside him)* He seems quite a good sort.

PEGGY. *(As she sits)* Yes.

CHARLES. Say, Pegs, old girl—this is not so good, is it?

PEGGY. No.

CHARLES. It's not my idea of a honeymoon, at all. Of course, if we were going to be together always, it wouldn't be so bad.

PEGGY. Please don't let's talk about it!

CHARLES. Sorry, Pegs. It's all so unfair, though —if only you could come——

PEGGY. I'm dying to come—you know that.

CHARLES. It's impossible—I may have to rough it a bit.

PEGGY. I wouldn't mind.

CHARLES. But I would. No, Pegs—I'm fit and well—it would be different for you.

PEGGY. I'm fit and well, too, Charlie.

CHARLES. *(Rising to down* R.) Why, I couldn't even raise the fare.

PEGGY. *(Sliding over to* R. *end of bench)* We might borrow it.

CHARLES. Do you really think we could?

PEGGY. Lots of people seem willing to lend money.

CHARLES. Do they?

PEGGY. *(On* R. *end of bench* C.*)* You can read about them in the papers.

CHARLES. *(At* R.*)* No, thanks—you stay with your mother, dear, till things take a turn.

PEGGY. *(Rising to him at* R.C.*)* All right, dear. I suppose you know best—and darling, no matter what happens, I love you. *(They embrace.)*

CHARLES. *(As they embrace)* Darling! *(They kiss.)*

TEDDIE. *(Raises ticket window* R. *as they kiss, and pokes his head out)* All change—all change! Line up on the right, please! Sorry, we're sold out of tickets to New York—nothing but Weehawken left! *(Seeing* CHARLES *and* PEGGY, *who have started a little apart)* Oh, I beg your pardon.

CHARLES. *(His arm about* PEGGY*)* That's all right—we're beginning to get a bit used to you.

TEDDIE. I believe somebody likes me. *(Sings in a cracked voice)* "Somebody loves me. I wonder who—I wonder who it can be——"

CHARLES. *(Crossing with* PEGGY *to down* L.*)* Oh, shut up!

TEDDIE. Don't you like my voice?

CHARLES. *(Turning at* L.*)* No, we don't—we think it's terrible.

TEDDIE. *(His head through ticket window* R.*)* W. E. A. F. signing off. Goodnight, everybody! *(Draws his head back and slams down window.)*

CHARLES. *(Sits on bench down* L. *with* PEGGY*)* That fellow's a lunatic!

(The door up R. *opens and* MISS BOURNE *enters, followed by* SAUL, ELSIE *and* RICHARD, *and* TEDDIE.*)*

MISS BOURNE. *(Crossing down and sits on bench* C. *with cage)* This is the worst-managed station

I've ever been at, in the whole course of my life. I shall most certainly write and complain about it to the company.

SAUL. *(Following to back of the table* C.*)* I wish you would, ma'm—darned if the conditions here ain't terrible! (ELSIE *crosses to up* L. TEDDIE *sits on bench up* R.*)*

CHARLES. What's the trouble?

RICHARD. *(Up* R.C.*)* The rain's coming through the roof, in there. We've had to clear out.

PEGGY. I'm getting hungry.

RICHARD. So am I. *(To* SAUL*)* Is there anything to eat here?

SAUL. No—not a bite.

MISS BOURNE. *(Looking into her parrot cage)* I'm sure I don't know what's the matter with my poor old Joey—he does seem depressed. Oh—he's laid an egg—— Now I shall have to call him Clara.

CHARLES. *(Crossing to* L.C. *and taking hold of the bench* C. *as if to move it)* Now, let's draw the bench up to the stove and make ourselves as comfortable as we can—— *(Realizing* MISS BOURNE *is on the bench)* Oh, I'm sorry—— May I? (MISS BOURNE *glares, and then rises, and he draws the bench over* L., *so that it is just beyond the table. Then* MISS BOURNE *sits on bench again,* L.C.*)*

RICHARD. Good idea! *(As* CHARLES *is moving bench, he crosses into ticket office* R., *and drags out swivel chair.)*

SAUL. *(Up* C. *as he sees* RICHARD *coming out with chair)* Oh, here—you can't take that chair out of there.

RICHARD. *(Crossing with chair to up* L.*)* What do you mean—I can't take it out?

SAUL. The Company put that chair in there for me to sell tickets on, and it can't come out.

RICHARD. *(As he gets up* L. *with chair)* It's out.

CHARLES. *(As he finishes moving bench to* L.C.*)*

That's better. *(Crosses to* PEGGY *down* L. *and both sit on bench down* L.)

(TEDDIE, *who has been trying to help, shoves table to* L. *so that it bumps the end of the bench* L.C. *on which* MISS BOURNE *is seated. She glares at him and shoves it back toward him. He gives it another shove to her, and she shoves it back once more.)*

MISS BOURNE. *(As she shoves table back the second time)* This is not a moving job.

TEDDIE. *(At* R.C. *by end of table)* Still hungry, ladies and gentlemen?

PEGGY. *(Seated on bench down* L. *by* CHARLES) Very!

TEDDIE. *(*R.C.*)* Oh, I'll soon fix that!

RICHARD. *(Up* L., *sits in straight chair by stove)* How?

CHARLES. *(Seated by* PEGGY *down* L.) Can you? (ELSIE *sits in swivel chair up* L.) } *(Together)*

TEDDIE. *(Crossing to ticket window* R.) Just coming, sir—— One moment, sir—— *(He raises window, and calls through it off* R.) Oh, Elmer! Six roast turkey and cranberry sauce—and draw six in the dark! *(He lets window drop, and turns back again to* R.C.) Sorry, sir, but the cook's gone to get her hair bobbed. There isn't a "shingle" thing left! But never mind—we'll go over to Childs!

MISS BOURNE. Young man, do you ever take anything in life seriously?

TEDDIE. *(*R.C.*)* Oh, yes.

MISS BOURNE. May I inquire what?

TEDDIE. *(In a stage whisper, leaning over end of table to her)* Whiskey!

MISS BOURNE. You're an impudent fellow!

TEDDIE. Flatterer! *(He sees the rice and con-*

fetti on floor R.C.) Oh, hello—hello—hello——
What have we here? *(He leans over to examine
floor.* MISS BOUNRE *also leans over to look.)* What
a perfect scream! Now, which of you is it? *(He
looks up into* MISS BOURNE'S *face. She straightens
up angrily.)* No—not guilty! *(Straightening up)*
And it can't be the parrot. *(Crosses back of table
to up* L.; *surveys* ELSIE *and* RICHARD*)* N-n-o—no
—hardly! *(Crosses a little down* L. *and surveys*
CHARLES *and* PEGGY, *who drops her head)* Ah!
That blush—that perturbed eye! Bogey—bogey! If
this isn't the funniest thing ever! Oh, wait till I
tell them about this at the club——

CHARLES. *(Down* L., *rising angrily)* Oh, hell!

TEDDIE. *Oh!* Oh, what you said! O-h-h!
Naughty—naughty—not in front of wifie. You're
not offended, are you?

CHARLES. Yes, I am!

TEDDIE. It's only my little joke. After all, it is
funny, isn't it?

CHARLES. No!

TEDDIE. No?

CHARLES. No!!

TEDDIE. Oh! Perhaps you're right. *(Crosses back
to down* R. *and sits.)*

SAUL. Well, seein' as how you've all decided to
stay here, I'll be off home!

RICHARD. *(Rising, to* SAUL *up* L.C.*)* You're going?

SAUL. You can stay here, if you've made up
your minds to, but not me!

RICHARD. I wish you'd stay—we might want
something.

SAUL. You'll want something, all right.

CHARLES. *(Rising, down* L.*)* Oh, stay—you know
where things are. We shan't forget you.

SAUL. You want *me* to stay here all night?

CHARLES. Why not?

SAUL. *(Coming down* R.C. *by end of table)* Me stay at Clear Vale Junction, all night?

RICHARD. That was the idea.

SAUL. See here, Mister, ain't you never heard tell about this here station?

CHARLES. No.

RICHARD. I never even knew it was here.

PEGGY. *(Seated down* L.*)* Well, what about it?

SAUL. It's haunted.

MISS BOURNE. *(Seated on bench* L.C.*)* Haunted? My God!

TEDDIE. *(Seated down* R.*)* Well, if this isn't absolutely too priceless—the station's haunted. *(Laughing.)*

SAUL. *(*R.C., *near table)* Go on—laugh.

TEDDIE. *(Still laughing)* May I? Thanks, I will.

SAUL. You'll laugh out of the other side of your face before morning.

RICHARD. You don't mean to say you believe in ghosts?

SAUL. I believe in *this* one. There ain't nobody in these parts what don't. No, sir—I wouldn't stay in this here station for all the money in the world—tonight of all nights!

RICHARD. You wouldn't be afraid to stay here with us, would you?

SAUL. Yes, I would!

RICHARD. What is the story? Anyway, before you go, you might tell us what to expect?

SAUL. *(Crossing up and looking out of window back* R.*)* No, I'll be getting home. It's a regular Maine Coast drizzle—it's goin' to pour cats and dogs any minute, and I don't want to get stalled in the mud.

CHARLES. Wait a minute—— You needn't go yet. Tell us about the ghost or ghosts? We want something to entertain us.

SAUL. *(*R.C.*)* Entertain you? My God! (RICH-

ARD *sits again in straight chair up* L. CHARLES *on bench down* L.)

RICHARD. Oh, come on!

TEDDIE. *(Seated down* R.) Yes, tell us about the ghosts?   *(Together)*

ELSIE. *(Seated on swivel chair up* L.) Please tell us?

SAUL. *(Coming a little more down* R.C.) All right, I'll tell you—but I warn you it ain't no pretty story, and I'd rather be goin' home. Twenty years ago, tonight, there was a man by the name of Ted Holmes, used to be in charge of this here station. Did you notice a bridge, just down below—— *(Pointing* L.)

CHARLES. Yes, I did.

RICHARD. Yes.

TEDDIE. I saw it.   *(Together)*

PEGGY. Yes.

ELSIE. Yes, I saw it.

SAUL. That's the bridge over Winslow's Creek. It's a swing bridge, and it used to be worked by a lever right out here on this very platform. In them days, quite big sized boats used to come up the Creek, after the china clay. They don't come up here no more!

RICHARD. Why not?

SAUL. Twenty years ago tonight there was a party of people started off on some sort of a jollification up to Rockland, and they chartered a special train to take them back home to Waldoboro, down the line. That was the only night train that ever run on these here lines. Ted Holmes was kept on duty that night to close the bridge, which was always left open for the clay boats to go out on the tide. It must have been eleven o'clock when they 'phoned from Rockland for Ted to close the bridge, that the special was a-startin'. Ted 'phones back as how he'd close the bridge that minute—and them was the last words he was ever heard to speak.

PEGGY. What happened?

SAUL. That was at eleven o'clock. Ted Holmes goes to that door there, and there it was that some sickness overcomes him, and he falls down on that very platform, just outside that very door—dead!

MISS BROUNE. How shocking!

PEGGY. Terrible!

SAUL. Outside that very door they found him, with the lamp still burnin' in his hand. It must have been eleven-thirty when the special left Rockland— and there was that bridge wide open, and Ted Holmes lyin' dead on the platform. On comes the train down the valley—on she comes, coming like hell, everyone being anxious to get home. On she comes, forty miles an hour she's makin'—poor old Ben Izaacs was a-drivin', and it seems as though something warned him. What it was, God only knows—but he claps on the brakes, and the train goes a-screamin' and a-tearin' through the station, with all the brakes on, and the whistles a-blowin' and then—crash!

RICHARD. Good God!

PEGGY. Oh, how awful!

CHARLES. Were there many killed?

SAUL. Six! Six killed outright—and two died after. By some miracle, poor Ben Izaacs was thrown clear. He makes his way out of the water, and back here to the station, his mind gone—and they say for hours he could be seen a-walkin' that platform, a-wavin' the lantern, and singin' "Rock of Ages." The next morning he died, an' it was a merciful release. Six bodies they brought up, and they laid 'em out in this very room. (*Coming a little down* R.C. *by front of table.*)

MISS BOURNE. What a horrible story!

SAUL. Well, I told you it was no pretty tale, ma'm—but you would have it!

RICHARD. But where does the haunting come in?

SAUL. *(Turning toward door up R.)* Maybe I've said enough—I don't want to scare the ladies.

ELSIE. Not a bit—it was a horrible thing, no doubt, but I don't see how it can frighten us. Please go on.

SAUL. *(Coming back to R.C.)* Ever since that night this station has been haunted.

CHARLES. Who by—Ted Holmes?

SAUL. Worse than that! Some nights the signal bell rings, and a train comes a-screamin' and a-tearin' through the station, with the brakes all on and the whistles a-blowin'!

RICHARD. Rot!

SAUL. *(R.C.)* I'm tellin' you it's the God's truth. I was kept late by a thunder storm, one night, not long back, and just as I get down the road I heard the signal bell ring, and then I saw her go through. I saw the flames from the engine—saw it with my own eyes.

CHARLES. I expect it's some freight train that's started this yarn.

SAUL. I'm telling you there ain't no trains runs on these tracks from ten o'clock at night till seven in the morning. Besides which, it never starts at Rockland, and it never runs into Waldoboro. If it's a natural thing, where does it come from—and where does it go?

CHARLES. Oh, rubbish!

SAUL. You don't believe me?

CHARLES. I'm afraid you're superstitious.

SAUL. All the folks around these parts run like the devil when they hear a train in the night. Do you know what they say it means to look on the ghost train?

RICHARD. No—what?

SAUL. Death!

RICHARD. Now you *are* talking rot.

SAUL. All right, Mister—— One night late, not long back, a tramp breaks into this waiting-room, and the next day they find him in here—dead! The doctor says as how he'd died of fear.

RICHARD. Coincidence!

SAUL. *(R.C.)* But that don't explain the train. Besides, they hear it tearing down the line. There was a man from a farm back here, started to walk to Rockland early one morning, to catch the boat for Bar Harbor, when he sees someone a-walkin' this platform, a-swingin' a lantern, and singing' "Rock of Ages"! No, you can stay here if you like, but not me. They say the dead walks this platform, and old Ben Izaacs leads them.

TEDDIE. *(Seated down R.)* I think this is all too perfectly priceless—I never heard anything so delightfully funny in all my life. *(Laughing.)*

SAUL. Funny?

TEDDIE. *(Rising)* You don't expect us to believe all that muck, do you?

SAUL. You'd better believe it—it's bad luck to scoff at the dead.

TEDDIE. *(Crossing to R.C. SAUL crosses down R.)* Do you know, all this reminds me of a story I once heard about a haunted police station, or fire station, or something—in London, or was it Manchester— no, I believe it was in Glasgow. Well, there was a man there one day, and he saw an old girl all dressed in brown, sitting on a seat—*(Directing his story to MISS BOURNE, L.C., who glares at him and shows much annoyance)* —and he said something to her, and then she disappeared—and he thought, "How lucky." And then he went around a corner, and there she was again, all dressed in brown, and he said to her—— Oh, it was a perfect scream

what he said. He said to her—he said—he said—
he said——

RICHARD. *(Seated up* L.; *impatiently)* Well, what
the devil did he say?

TEDDIE. He said—— Oh, it was the funniest
thing what he said—he said—he said—— Well,
now, I'm afraid it's quite escaped me for the moment just what he did say, but I know it was a
perfect scream.

SAUL. You ought to be ashamed of yourself.

TEDDIE. Now don't get angry, old thing! Man
to man, you know, *your* story was rather steep.
(Turning toward MISS BOURNE, *who rises and
glares at him as if daring him to tell it)* But never
mind—it reminds me of another story about a
clergyman, and he'd just gotten married, and he'd
married a most unpleasant woman, and they were
walking along from the church to the honeymoon,
and he had the most unpleasant lady's handbag in
one hand, and he said to her—he said—he said——
(As MISS BOURNE *moves closer and glares)* No—
I don't think so. *(Turns away and crosses to* R.
SAUL *crosses up* R.C.*)*

MISS BOURNE. *(At* C.*)* I shall never travel on
this line again—they only seem to specialize in
idiots! *(To* SAUL*)* Isn't there any proper system
of signalling?

SAUL. It's only a single track, ma'm, and back
where the accident happened the line was just
opened. Things are different now, and the swing
bridge is never opened.

TEDDIE. *(Seated down* R.*)* What did you say
that jolly old lever on the platform was for, then?

SAUL. That works the switch to the siding that
runs up to the old lumber mill—a matter of a hun-
dred yards.

RICHARD. *(Rising; crossing to up* L.C.*)* Well,
Station Master, your story has been very entertain-

ing, but a bit gruesome. I'm sorry I can't believe it all, but—— *(A FACE lighted up by a green flash is seen for an instant at window up* L.)

PEGGY. *(Seated down* L., *seeing face at window, rises with a scream)* A-a-ah! Look! (ALL *rise quickly.)*

RICHARD. *(Up* L.C.*)* What! ⎫
CHARLES. *(Down* L.*)* What! ⎬ *(Together)*
MISS BOURNE. *(Down* C.*)* Ah! ⎭

PEGGY. I saw someone looking in through that window. *(The* MEN *exchange a look and then cross up.* CHARLES *opens* C. *door and exits, followed by* RICHARD *and* TEDDIE. SAUL *follows up to door* C., *then crosses and looks off through ticket office door* R.; *then exits* R.*)*

CHARLES. *(Returning, crosses to* PEGGY*)* No one about, Pegs!

RICHARD. *(Following him in, goes to up* L.*)* Not a soul! (TEDDIE *follows in and crosses to down* R.*)*

ELSIE. *(Standing by window up* L.C.*)* Must have been your imagination, I guess.

PEGGY. *(To* MISS BOURNE, *who has seated herself again on bench* L.C.*)* I saw it most distinctly!

MISS BOURNE. This really is a most unpleasant station.

TEDDIE. One of those jolly old ghosts, perhaps.

RICHARD. Shut up, you fool.

TEDDIE. *(Seated down* R.*)* Sorry!

CHARLES. *(Down* L.*)* It must have been your imagination, Pegs.

PEGGY. *(Down* L. *by* CHARLES*)* Perhaps so—— I'm sorry if I startled you.

ELSIE. *(Up* L.C.*)* I wasn't afraid at all!

RICHARD. *(Up* L.*)* That's the worst of ghost stories, Mrs. Murdock. They are apt to make the best of us jumpy, though most of us haven't the moral courage to own up to it.

ELSIE. *(Sharply)* Thank you.

RICHARD. I wasn't referring to you. (SAUL *enters from up* R.) Oh, I say, Station Master, can't you get us some more coal? This fire is almost out.

SAUL. Why, we ain't got a bit left, sir. We expect some in from Rockland tomorrow.

MISS BOURNE. It's really awfully cold and damp. It'll about finish my old bird—the egg'll be frozen—and all this trouble for nothing!

TEDDIE. *(Rising; to* R.C.*)* Oh, do cheer up, people—it's sure to be worse.

MISS BOURNE. *(Rising; to him* R.C. *She has cage with her)* It's all very well for you to talk, young man—you have landed us in this most unpleasant situation, and instead of expressing regret—no—no—no—no! *(She advances to him, backing him up till he sits on chair down* R.*)* All you can do is to sit and make fun of us. You're an impudent, ill-mannered puppy, sir. My poor sister will be sitting up all night for me, and here I am in a cold railway station, with ghosts—ghosts and things all over the place—and all you can do is to sit there and laugh. I hate the sight of you—I will not stop in the room another moment with you. Try and lead a better life—and don't come near me. *(She strikes his extended hand a sharp blow, takes cage and crosses up into ticket office up* R. *She continues off* R.*)* Oh—— Oh—— Oh! Look here! *(Comes back into room, pointing off* R.*)*

CHARLES. *(Crossing to her up* R.*)* What's the matter?

MISS BOURNE. *(Pointing off* R.*)* I saw something move in there.

CHARLES. *(Goes off up* R. *and immediately returns)* Why, that's only a sack of potatoes, on the floor.

MISS BOURNE. *(Giving her skirts a hitch)* Oh, I do so hate potatoes! *(Drops on bench up* R.*)*

ELSIE. *(Crosses and sits beside her)* It's all right, Miss Bourne—really it is.

SAUL. Well, I'll get my lantern, and be off home.

RICHARD. Wait a minute?

SAUL. No, sir! I wouldn't stay here another minute—not for a thousand dollars! I know too much about this station!

CHARLES. Can't you see you're frightening the ladies?

SAUL. Well, that ain't my fault. I warned you when you first come that Clear Vale Junction was no pleasant place to spend the night. If you'll take my advice, you'll set out for the farm, even now. *(Exits up R. Gets bicycle lamp, and comes back.)*

RICHARD. We'll do no such thing!

ELSIE. I should think not. We're not going to catch our deaths of cold because of a stupid ghost story.

SAUL. *(Crossing with bicycle lamp to behind table C., preparing to light it)* All right, ma'm. I've done my best, but I ain't going to risk no more—I've got a family depending on me.

RICHARD. All right, then—go and be damned to you, if you're afraid.

SAUL. I am afraid, and I ain't ashamed to own it.

CHARLES. Where's your motorcycle?

SAUL. Outside, under the shed. Have you got a match, sir?

CHARLES. *(Handing him box of matches)* Yes, here you are.

SAUL. *(Taking matches)* Thank you, sir. *(As he is lighting his lamp at C., behind table)* My Presto-Light went back on me. It's a good thing I got my lantern. *(Handing back matches)* Thank you, sir. *(He takes his lamp and backs up to door C.)* Well, I'll be back here at seven in the morning. And if you'll take my advice you'll stay in here.

And if you should hear a train—for God's sake don't go running out to look at it.

RICHARD. *(Little up* L.C.*)* Oh, stop talking like an old woman. If you believe in your ghost, well and good. We don't—understand?

SAUL. *(Up* C. *by door)* All right!

RICHARD. All right—clear out!

SAUL. *(Opening door up* C.*)* Good night! *(Exits* C., *closing door.)*

RICHARD. Good night!

TEDDIE. *(Crossing to door up* C., *calling after* SAUL *through the door)* Good night, old thing, and a pleasant ride to you—I hope you get jolly well soaked! And thanks for the "Bogey" ride. *(Turning down to swivel chair* L.C.*)* Cheery old soul—that chap!

RICHARD. *(Coming down* C. *to table)* Now, then, we'd better make some arrangements for the night. The ladies had better sleep in here—it's drier than the ticket office.

MISS BOURNE. *(On bench up* R.*)* Sleep in here—What a pleasant death!

RICHARD. *(Coming to* R. *end of table)* Look here, you fellows. Help me move this table. Somebody may be able to rest on this.

(CHARLES *comes to front of table,* TEDDIE *to* L. *of it, and they start to move it up* L. ELSIE *crosses down to front of table and takes her bag, crossing with it to down* L., *where she places it under bench.* PEGGY *crosses to table and takes her bag up* L. *to behind stove, and pulls chair up* L. *back to* L., *out of the way. As the* MEN *start with table,* TEDDIE *trips backward into swivel chair* L.C. *and twirls about in it.)*

TEDDIE. *(Whirling about in swivel chair* L.C.*)* Oh, I say—look at this!

RICHARD. *(As they are moving table)* Come on and make yourself useful, for once in your life.

TEDDIE. *(As they get the table up L.)* If you want cheering up, I can amuse you with a whistling solo. *(They ad lib. lines and business till table is placed under the window up L. at back.)*

CHARLES. *(Up L., front of table, as they finish placing it)* I say, what fools we are!

RICHARD. *(Up L.C. near door C.)* What's the matter?

CHARLES. We never cold that old fellow to bring us any food when he comes back.

ELSIE. *(Down L.)* He may think of it.

CHARLES. I doubt it.   *(WARN Curtain.)*

RICHARD. So do I.

MISS BOURNE. *(On bench up R.)* He's a very disobliging man. I'm going to report him to the company. *(BUMP of a body outside door C.)* What's that?

CHARLES. *(Crossing to R. side of door up C.)* Goodness knows! *(He opens door and SAUL's body falls face forward into the room. RICHARD, up L.C., and CHARLES, up R.C., catch him as he falls forward and lay him down up and down stage, face down, his hand with the lamp extended so that the lamp shines straight front.)*

RICHARD. *(As they catch him)* What the devil?

PEGGY. *(L. near stove)* Is he ill?

MISS BOURNE. *(Up R.)* Sure he can't be——

ELSIE. *(Down L., screams and points to lantern in SAUL's hand)* A-h-h!! *(START TELE-GRAPH.)*

RICHARD. What? What's the matter?

ELSIE. Look! Look!

RICHARD. What?

ELSIE. Look! The lamp!

RICHARD. Well?

ELSIE. *(Down L.)* Don't you remember—"Outside the door, they found him, with the lamp still burning in his hand!"

RICHARD. *(Up* L.C.*)* What's the time?

CHARLES. *(Up* R.C., *looking at wrist watch)* Eleven o'clock!

RICHARD. *(As the Curtain is coming down)* Good God!

CURTAIN

CALLS: *First Call—Picture.*

ALL OTHER CALLS: *Company.*

ACT TWO

SCENE: *The same as Act I.*

The table which was down C. *at the beginning of Act I is now against the back wall up* L. *below the window. The bench which was in front of the table before has also been moved and is now in front of the table up* L. *The swivel chair which was brought on from off up* R. *is now placed at* L.C. *All the cushions and rugs which were brought on by the various characters during Act I are now upon the table, as is* CHARLES' *coat and hat. The bags have all been placed under the table.* RICHARD'S *coat and hat are hanging in the corner up* R. *behind ticket office door.* ELSIE'S *and* PEGGY'S *coats and hats are hanging on wall* L., *behind the stove.*

TIME: *Fifteen minutes later. Eleven-fifteen, the same night.*

AT RISE: *The room is lighted as at beginning of Act I. The stove door is now open, and the red glow shines out more clearly. Doors up* C. *and up* R. *are closed, but ticket office window is open. As Curtain rises there is heard the steady fall of the RAIN outside, and when the door* C. *is opened, rainfall effect is seen on the back drop. It is interspersed from time to time with gusts of WIND, flashes of LIGHTNING, and the rumble of THUNDER. There are discovered* MISS BOURNE, *seated in swivel chair* L.C.,

PEGGY, *who is seated on* L. *end of bench in front of table up* L., *and* ELSIE, *who is seated on corner of table up* L.C., *near door, trying with shaking hands to light a cigarette.*

ELSIE. *(Strikes a match which does not light)* Darn! *(She strikes another, which also does not light)* Damn!

PEGGY. *(Rising up* L.*)* Your hand is shaking— Let me light it for you.

ELSIE. Thank you. My hand is perfectly steady. These matches are beastly. *(She strikes another match and is finally successful.)*

MISS BOURNE. However you can smoke at a time like this, I don't know. It's awful!

PEGGY. *(Crosses to* L. *of* MISS BOURNE*)* A cigarette is rather soothing when the nerves are upset.

ELSIE. My nerves are perfectly normal.

MISS BOURNE. I'm sure I don't know what is going to happen to us.

PEGGY. *(Soothingly)* Nothing, Miss Bourne— you forget there are *three* men with us.

MISS BOURNE. Yes, but there were *four* men with us, just now.

ELSIE. Try not to think about it.

MISS BOURNE. I do try not to think about it. He lay there—— Oh—it was shocking! *(She breaks down.)*

PEGGY. *(*L. *of* MISS BOURNE, L.C. *Tries to comfort her)* Please, Miss Bourne—don't give way!

MISS BOURNE. To think that such a thing should happen to me. I've read of things in the newspapers at times—terrible things—but they always seemed a long way off, and never seemed real. Living with my dear sister for so many years, there never seemed to be any possibility of anything terrible happening to us.

PEGGY. But nothing has happened to you.

MISS BOURNE. Nothing happened? My dear child —how can you say such a thing? I shall never be the same woman again. *(Almost breaks down again.)*

ELSIE. You must try and pull yourself together.

MISS BOURNE. I'll try—I'll try—— I think I am a little bit better. In fact, I'm not as nervous as I was—— (CHARLES *rattles latch of door up* R. *from outside as he opens it. The* WOMEN *are all startled.)* What's that?

TEDDIE. *(Pokes his head out of ticket office window at* R.*)* It's all right—it's only us.

(CHARLES *enters up* R., *followed by* RICHARD *and* TEDDIE. PEGGY *crosses and meets* CHARLES *up* R.C. *and they cross down* R., *where she sits, with* CHARLES *on the arm of her chair.* RICHARD *crosses down* C. *and* TEDDIE *goes up and lies on bench up* L.*)*

RICHARD. *(As he enters and crossing down* C.*)* Now, ladies, this is a very unpleasant business, and has given us all a bit of a jar, but we must try not to take it too seriously. *(*ELSIE *crosses up* L.C. *and sits, bench by table; smokes a cigarette.* PEGGY *and* CHARLES *cross and sit down* R.*)*

MISS BOURNE. *(Seated swivel chair* L.C.*)* Can't we get away somewhere?

RICHARD. I wish we could, but it's raining harder than ever. Coming down in sheets. Besides, there's nothing to be afraid of now—we've put that poor fellow in the other room, and locked the door. Let's try and forget about it.

MISS BOURNE. Forget!

RICHARD. We must be sensible. There's hardly a house in America where someone hasn't died— hardly a station where someone hasn't met with an accident. And as for that poor fellow in there—

people do die suddenly sometimes, and we have the consolation of knowing that he was spared any pain or suffering.

PEGGY. *(Seated down* R.*)* Then you don't think his death had anything to do with the story he told us?

RICHARD. My dear lady—dismiss that from your mind. It was just a coincidence.

TEDDIE. *(Rising from bench up* R. *and crossing down* R.C.*)* And a jolly strange thing, wasn't it? It was just what he said happened—every detail!

CHARLES. *(Seated on arm of* PEGGY'S *chair)* Shut up!

TEDDIE. That's all very well, old thing—but I think I'm entitled to my opinion, as well as anyone else.

CHARLES. You're not entitled to frighten people.

TEDDIE. There was no such idea in my head. I was only just thinking of a story I once heard, about some people who spent the night in a haunted mill—or shop—or something, and just as the clock was striking midnight——

RICHARD. We don't want that story. *(Crosses back of* MISS BOURNE *to* L., *near stove.)*

TEDDIE. All right. Don't get peeved about it, old thing. I don't believe in ghosts myself—I think the whole thing is all rather a scream—but still, on the other hand, so did all those other people who spent the night in that haunted mill, or shop. *(Addressing himself to* MISS BOURNE, L.C., *who shrinks back)* Do you know, they hadn't been there more than half an hour when they saw the most horrible——

CHARLES. *(Crossing threateningly toward him up* R.*)* Will you shut up?

TEDDIE. *(Looking about him at the others)* Very well, I will—and just for that I shan't tell you the story at all. *(Sits again on bench up* R.*)*

MISS BOURNE. *(Seated swivel chair* L.C.*)* I'm sure there is some terrible, supernatural force at work.

RICHARD. *(Near stove)* Nonsense!

MISS BOURNE. That's what you said before, and yet look what happened.

RICHARD. I said it was pure coincidence.

CHARLES. *(Near ticket window)* It's no good worrying about it, Miss Bourne.

MISS BOURNE. Then there was that face at the window.

PEGGY. That might have been only my imagination.

MISS BOURNE. And it might not. I'm perfectly sure I saw something move in the other room. *(Ticket window falls with a bang)* Oh! Oh! *(They all start.* ELSIE *jumps to her feet up* L.C. TEDDY *up* R. PEGGY, *with a scream, runs into* CHARLES' *arms.)*

CHARLES. *(Looks hesitantly at ticket window; reassures* PEGGY*)* It's nothing—it only flopped down.

RICHARD. *(Crossing to* C.*)* Only the ticket window falling—nothing supernatural about that.

TEDDIE. *(Rising and crossing down* R.C.*)* That reminds me of something—— Whatever is it? Oh, yes, I know. It was in England. *(To* RICHARD*)* Have you ever been in England?

RICHARD. Yes, I go there for several months, every year, on business.

TEDDIE. Oh, well, then, you'll appreciate this. It was at Nottingham—— No, it was Golder's Green—

RICHARD. I've never been at that station.

TEDDIE. Oh, I don't mean the station—I mean the Crematorium——

PEGGY. *(Sitting down* R. *with a shudder)* O-h-h!

TEDDIE. *(Indicating with a movement toward the*

ticket window) You know how they push the
bodies——

RICHARD. Once and for all, we don't want that
story.

TEDDIE. *(Indicating window once more)* I was
only saying that they only push the bodies——

RICHARD. Will you shut up?

TEDDIE. You're a difficult crowd to entertain.
(Crosses to bench up R. and sits.)

MISS BOURNE. *(Seated L.C.)* Oh, my goodness—
whatever shall we do?

CHARLES. *(Down R. by PEGGY)* We must pull
ourselves together, that's what we must do.

MISS BOURNE. Don't you believe in ghosts, young
man?

CHARLES. *(Coming toward her to C.)* I don't believe in them, and I don't disbelieve in them.

MISS BOURNE. Whatever do you mean?

CHARLES. I try to be open-minded on the subject. I've never had the slightest reason to believe
in anything supernatural myself, but I wouldn't en-
tirely disbelieve the testimony of other people. I
may not be Sir Oliver Lodge, nor Conan Doyle, but
I suppose things often do happen to people, that
cannot be explained.

MISS BOURNE. There you are, you see.

CHARLES. But all this is beside the point—nothing supernatural has happened here.

MISS BOURNE. But it might! Suppose that train
should come—— Whatever should we do?

CHARLES. What train?

MISS BOURNE. Why, the ghost train we spoke of.

CHARLES. Oh, that was just a story. *(Crosses
back to PEGGY.)*

MISS BOURNE. But you never know, you know.

PEGGY. *(Down R., rises quickly)* Listen!

CHARLES. What is it?

PEGGY. Listen! Listen! *(A slight pause, while* ALL *listen.)*

RICHARD. *(A little up* L.*)* Well?

PEGGY. I could have sworn I heard a step outside!

TEDDIE. *(Takes a step down)* A step outside?

RICHARD. *(Coming a step toward* C.*)* A step outside!

CHARLES. You're not usually so nervous, Pegs.

PEGGY. I'm absolutely certain, Charlie.

TEDDIE. Oh, we'll soon settle that. *(Crosses and opens door* C., *goes out and looks about outside in front of door, then tiptoes very mysteriously back down* C., *his finger to his lips, and he leans forward with an air of great secrecy)* Nobody!

MISS BOURNE. *(Rising in exasperation)* They should lay poison down for you. Why don't you shut the door? Do you want things to get in at us? *(*PEGGY *crosses to her at* L.C. *as she sits and breaks down, sobbing.* RICHARD *also comes down to* L. *of her.* TEDDIE *crosses and slams* C. *door shut, then sits again up* R.; *opens newspaper.)*

PEGGY. *(By* MISS BOURNE*)* Come, now, Miss Bourne—there's nothing to be frightened about. It was another mistake of mine, that's all.

MISS BOURNE. Oh, I feel so ill—I'm sure I'm going to faint.

TEDDIE. *(Rising and coming down* R.C., *has newspaper under his arm)* Oh, I've just had a brain wave! *(Taking flask from his pocket and holding it up)* I forgot all about this.

RICHARD. *(Crossing to* C. *of him)* What is it?

TEDDIE. Brandy!

RICHARD. *(Taking flask)* Brandy! The very thing! *(Crosses in front of* MISS BOURNE *to* L. *of her, taking cup off flask)* Come on, Miss Bourne— have a little of this—brandy!

MISS BOURNE. *(Seated* L.C.*)* Oh, no—no! I

couldn't think of it—I couldn't. *(Sniffing drink which* RICHARD *has poured)* I'm a strict toteetlet!

PEGGY. *(L.C. by her)* But this is different, Miss Bourne—this is medicine.

MISS BOURNE. No—no—you're very kind—but—certainly not.

RICHARD. *(Holds drink out for her)* Oh, come on!

MISS BOURNE. Whatever would the parson say?

RICHARD. He'd say you had been very sensible.

MISS BOURNE. Do you think so—really? *(Sniffs again.)*

RICHARD. I'm sure of it!

MISS BOURNE. *(Looks up at him with a slight wink)* Then, just a spot. *(She takes up cup and drinks a little, smacking her lips after)* U-g-h! Now I've broken my what-you-may-call-it—my pledge! (RICHARD *reaches for the cup. She draws it away from him)* Do you know, that isn't half as bad as I imagined? *(She finishes the cup.)*

RICHARD. Well, have a drop more?

MISS BOURNE. Do you think I ought?

RICHARD. Certainly! *(He holds out flask.)*

MISS BOURNE. Then just a sip. (RICHARD *pours another drink, then as* TEDDIE *speaks, hands her the flask.)*

TEDDIE. *(At* R.C., *looking at paper)* I say!

RICHARD. Well? }
CHARLES. Well! }   *(Together)*

TEDDIE. Couldn't we all do this cross-word puzzle?

RICHARD. *(Crosses front to* C.) What are you going to do a crossword puzzle with? (CHARLES *crosses to* R.C., *beside* TEDDIE. PEGGY *crosses around back to down* R. *by* CHARLES. MISS BOURNE, *during the following, pours and drinks several drinks from the cup, then after a side glance to see she is not observed, empties the flask by drinking from it.)*

TEDDIE. With a piece of paper, and a pencil with

a rubber on it. *(Indicating on paper)* Look here—number one across—"Our silent president." *(Suddenly, after thinking for a moment)* Washington!

RICHARD. *(With a laugh)* Washington? Why, he's dead!

TEDDIE. Well, then he's silent, isn't he?

RICHARD. *(Disgustedly, takes paper from* TEDDIE *at* C.*)* Here, let's see—number six, down, "Drunk at Christmas"—six letters——

TEDDIE. *(*R.C.*, suddenly)* Father! (RICHARD *disgustedly hands paper back to him)* Oh, here's one—"A common cereal"—— A common—— *(Suddenly)* The Green Hat!

RICHARD. *(Disgusted)* Oh, don't be a fool, man!

CHARLES. And when you speak don't speak so suddenly.

TEDDIE. I didn't—— When did I speak suddenly? Oh, yes, I remember—I did speak suddenly, didn't I? *(Looking about at them)* You don't seem to like me very much, do you?

RICHARD. *(Crossing to* MISS BOURNE, *who by now is quite affected by the drinks)* Well, Miss Bourne—feel better now?

MISS BOURNE. *(Hastily putting cup back on flask)* O-o-h, yes—I think I do feel a little better.

RICHARD. *(Taking flask and turning back to* C.*)* I thought that would revive you. *(Taking off cup and looking at flask, seeing it empty)* Good Lord! *(Hands flask to* TEDDIE.*)*

TEDDIE. *(Seeing flask empty)* My hat!

CHARLES. *(Down* R.*)* What is it now?

TEDDIE. *(Inverting and showing the empty flask)* What is it now? Empty—the blooming flask is empty.

CHARLES. What of it?

TEDDIE. What of it? It was full just now—simply packed with brandy—full to the rotten brim.

RICHARD. Whew! *(They* ALL *turn and look at*

Miss Bourne, *who is by now quite tipsy)* Well, it won't do her any harm.

Teddie. It won't do me any good. (Miss Bourne *now swings tipsily back and forth in swivel chair, crosses and uncrosses her knees, puts her glove on the wrong hand, searches for the other glove, finally, finds it on floor and recovers it and puts it on, while they all watch her, and at last swings around in chair toward them, becoming voluble.)*

Miss Bourne. *(Seated chair L.C., swinging to C. toward them)* Do you know—that's marvelous stuff. Do y'know—all my troubles have gone. Gone —on the wings of the blast—blast! I don't mean wickedness—I mean wind.

Charles. *(With a laugh)* Good Lord!

Peggy. *(Also laughing)* Is she——?

Charles. I'm afraid she is!

Teddie. *(*R.C.*)* Utterly plastered!

Charles. *(Crossing to RICHARD C.)* I say, what are we going to do?

Richard. *(With a look at Miss Bourne)* Well, somebody had better do something.

Charles. *(Crosses front to L. of Miss Bourne and leans over her)* Miss Bourne—Miss Bourne! (Peggy *crosses to R. of Miss Bourne.)*

Miss Bourne. *(Seated L.C., looking up at* Charles*)* Don't bite me.

Charles. Wouldn't you like to lie down? (Ted-DIE *crosses; sits down R.)*

Miss Bourne. *(Gets very dignified; pushes* Charles *away)* Young man! You forget yourself. *(Turns to* Peggy *at her R.)* I say, m'dear— do you know this young man?

Peggy. Why, yes—that's my husband.

Miss Bourne. *(Very positively)* Well, he's no good.

Elsie. *(Seated on bench up L.C.)* Disgusting!

Richard. Don't be absurd, Elsie. It was only an

accident. *(Crosses to* R. *of* MISS BOURNE *as* PEGGY *crosses around back to down* L., *where she sits on chair below stove)* Now, then, Miss Bourne—come along. (RICHARD *and* CHARLES *attempt to get her to her feet, and as they seem to be about to succeed, she slides from the chair to a sitting position on the floor, facing front, her hands resting on her knees.* RICHARD *bends over and pats her hand as he speaks)* Now come along, birdie—you mustn't sit there.

MISS BOURNE. *(Seated on floor, pats his hand in return)* Why not?

RICHARD. Because the floor's too hard.

MISS BOURNE. *(Very definitely)* That's my business.

RICHARD. Come on, now—get up.

MISS BOURNE. I won't.

RICHARD. Why not?

MISS BOURNE. Because I want to be Queen of the May.

RICHARD. Come on, now—you're going to get up. (RICHARD *and* CHARLES *get her to her feet. As she gets upright she pitches forward, and is saved from falling on her face by* RICHARD, *who catches her on his extended arm, and they now guide her till she gets back of the chair* L.C. ELSIE *rises and crosses up* R.)

CHARLES. *(*L. *of* MISS BOURNE*)* Now, Mrs. Bourne——

MISS BOURNE. I'm not Mrs. Bourne! It's a mistake, Mrs. Bourne—I'm not a mistake, but I'm not Mrs. Bourne! I'm an unmarried lady—spinster— *(Turns to* RICHARD *at her* R.) —maiden lady! You've met 'em?

RICHARD. Yes.

MISS BOURNE. Oh, you're lucky. Do you know, I've had my chances—oh, yes, I've had my chances —but I wouldn't take 'em. No—'cause I took the gypsy's warning.

RICHARD. Wise girl!

MISS BOURNE. *(Turns to CHARLES)* But I don't mind telling you, my blue-eyed boy—that I was not neglected in my youth. *(She punctuates by slapping his shoulders and face.)*

RICHARD. Come along now, Miss Bourne. *(With some difficulty they get her to a sitting position on the edge of the table up L. PEGGY rises and crosses up to L. end of table to help, closing stove door as she passes)* Push!

MISS BOURNE. *(Seated on edge of table up L.)* Don't push—I'm not a wheel-barrow. *(Sidling toward RICHARD, who leans against corner of table beside her)* I wish I'd met you earlier—— Oh, I do—but I'll tell you what I'll do—I'll give you Clara —egg and all! *(She slumps forward and passes out. They lay her out on the table, and PEGGY and CHARLES arrange her on the cushions and cover her with rugs, coats, etc., PEGGY placing the vacuum bottle on L. end of table as they finish.)*

RICHARD. *(After they have placed MISS BOURNE on table, crossing to ELSIE, up R.)* Feel better now?

ELSIE. *(Crossing down C.)* I wasn't aware that I was ill!

RICHARD. *(Following down to R.C.)* You know what I mean—just now!

ELSIE. *(Turning)* Well?

RICHARD. When we found that fellow dead I was anxious about you—you seemed quite hysterical.

ELSIE. I lost my head for a moment—that was all. I wasn't really afraid.

RICHARD. Of course! *I* was here, wasn't I?

ELSIE. *(Quickly)* Yes. *(Recovering herself)* It would have been all the same if you hadn't been here.

RICHARD. Are you sure?

ELSIE. I've told you I don't need protection.

RICHARD. Then—that separation idea still goes?

ELSIE. Of course! Why not?

RICHARD. I don't know—I thought perhaps you might have changed your mind.

ELSIE. You know I never change my mind. *(Crosses to down L.)*   *(START WIND.)*

RICHARD. *(Making a start to follow her)* See here, Elsie——

CHARLES. *(Crossing down to RICHARD C.)* It was funny, wasn't it—her getting lit up as easy as that?

RICHARD. She emptied the flask!

PEGGY. *(By table)* Perhaps it's as well for the poor soul—she might not wake up until it's daylight.

TEDDIE. *(Comes a little down R.C.)* Damned hard lines on me! I didn't reckon on her swigging the entire issue. Well, I think I might as well snatch forty winks, too—if you're sure you can manage without my advice.

RICHARD. We'll manage somehow.

TEDDIE. *(Turning back to bench up R.)* Thanks frightfully. *(Stretches himself out on bench.)*

RICHARD. *(With a start toward L.)* That's not a bad idea!

CHARLES. *(At C., stopping him)* Wait a bit—I've just thought of something.

RICHARD. Well?

CHARLES. There must be a telephone here, connecting with the other station.

RICHARD. No good! It seems to be out of order. I tried that ten minutes ago. *(Turns away to R.C.)*

CHARLES. That settles that. *(Turns away to L.C. There is a sudden KNOCK at door up C. ALL are startled. PEGGY crosses a little down L. by stove. ELSIE rises quickly down R.)*

(JULIA PRICE, attired in evening gown and cloak,

enters C. *quickly, closing door and standing against it.)*

CHARLES. *(Turns as* JULIA *enters)*
Hello!
RICHARD. *(Turning also)* Who are
you? } *(Together)*

JULIA. Tell me—has it come?

CHARLES. I beg your pardon? *(STOP WIND.)*

JULIA. Has it come?

CHARLES. I'm afraid I don't quite follow you.

JULIA. You know—you must know.

RICHARD. I don't think we do! *(LIGHTS DOWN.)*

JULIA. *(Coming a few steps down toward* RICHARD, R.C.*)* Listen to me—I want you to help me. Will you help me?

RICHARD. Of course—but what's the matter?

JULIA. Hide me from them. Hide me—please.

RICHARD. Hide you? From whom?

JULIA. From them!

RICHARD. But—who are they?

JULIA. You must help me. Don't let them take me back—I can't go back—I can't.

PRICE. *(His VOICE heard in the distance off* c. *to* R.*)* Julia! Julia!   *(START WIND.)*

JULIA. What shall I do? They'll take me back again—— Help me.

CHARLES. That's all right—nobody's going to hurt you.

JULIA. Then let me hide in there. *(Starts for door up* R.*)*

RICHARD. *(Barring her way)* No—no! Not in there!

JULIA. Then where can I go?

RICHARD. Anywhere—but in there!

PRICE. *(His VOICE heard off* c. *to* R. *and nearer)* Julia! Julia!

JULIA. They're coming, I tell you.

PEGGY. *(At* L. *by stove)* It's all right.

JULIA. It's not all right. (JULIA *runs quickly up* C. *and faces the door, holding it closed, then with her face to door, swinging around with it as it opens, so that she is hidden behind the open door.)*

(Door is opened from outside by HERBERT PRICE, *who enters to down* R.C., *followed by* JOHN STERLING, *who stops a little up* L.C. *Both are in dinner clothes.)*

STERLING. *(As he enters)* Who the blazes are you people?

RICHARD. *(Who has dropped a little back to* R.) That's just what I was going to ask you?

PRICE. We are looking for my niece. Have you seen a young lady about here? We have every reason to believe she would come to this station.

RICHARD. Then she has run away from you?

PRICE. In a way—yes! Have you seen her?

CHARLES. *(Who has drawn back to* L., *near* PEGGY) But why should she run away? Why should she come here?

PRICE. That is not a matter I care to discuss with strangers!

CHARLES. In that case, I'm afraid we can't help you! *(LIGHTNING—THUNDER.)*

STERLING. *(*L.C.*)* She's here somewhere, Price —I know that! Look in the other room!

PRICE. Very well! *(Turns to door* R. RICHARD *bars his way.)*

RICHARD. *(At* L. *quickly)* Stop! You can't go in there!

PRICE. *(Stopping* R.C.*)* And why not?

CHARLES. Because—there's something we must explain.

PRICE. So she's there! *(Turns again toward* R.)

CHARLES. No!

PRICE. *(Coming a little back toward* C. *toward* CHARLES*)* I'm sorry, but I don't believe you. You are doing a very foolish thing to interfere in this matter. *(Turns to door* R. *again.)*

RICHARD. *(Bars his way up* R.C.*)* She's not in there.

CHARLES. I give you my word of honor.

PRICE. Not good enough! Shut that door, Sterling. *(Indicates door* C.*)*

STERLING. *(*L.C. *Crosses up and closes door* C.*)* Certainly!

PRICE. *(*R.C. *continuing)* I mean to get to the bottom of this.

STERLING. *(As he closes door up* C., *sees* JULIA *crouching in terror behind it, she has dropped her cloak on end of bench up* R.*)* Hello!

PRICE. So there you are, Julia!

JULIA. It's no good—I can't go back. You know I can't.

STERLING. *(Up* L.C.*)* Come along, Julia—let's get away from here. *(Moves a little toward her.)*

JULIA. *(Coming quickly a little down* C.*)* No! No! I can't!

PRICE. Be sensible, Julia!

JULIA. What's the use of talking—I must stay here. I can't help myself.

PRICE. *(Crosses to her* R.; *attempts to seize her)* That's enough of this.

JULIA. *(Tears herself away.* RICHARD *comes a little down* R.*)* Go away! Go away!

PRICE. Damn it all!

STERLING. See here, Price—leave her to me.

PRICE. If she won't come, we must take her. *(Makes another movement toward her.* JULIA *circles around in front of him and crosses to* RICHARD *down* R., *who puts his arm protectingly over her shoulder.)*

RICHARD. You will pardon me, but this lady has put herself under our protection.

PRICE. *(Angrily)* Who the devil asked you to interfere—kindly keep out of this.

RICHARD. *(Down R., places JULIA below him)* You are not going to take this lady away against her will.

PRICE. *(At C.)* Mind your own business.

CHARLES. *(At L.)* This is our business.

STERLING. *(Up L.C. Crossing down R.C. to JULIA)* You'd better explain to them, Price—it's no good trying to ride roughshod, in a case like this. *(Turning to JULIA)* Come, dear, let's sit down over here. *(JULIA allows him to lead her across to swivel chair L.C., where she sits. ELSIE sits on bench down L. CHARLES stands between PEGGY at L. by stove and JULIA at L.C.)*

PRICE. *(Coming to C.)* Have you people heard the story about this place?

CHARLES. We heard the ghost story—something about this station being haunted. That's the one, I suppose?

PRICE. Yes. Please don't let my niece worry you. She's—well, she suffers from—er—well—delusions, at times.

RICHARD. *(Coming a little R.C.)* You mean she's——?

PRICE. Well, hardly that. It's all this infernal ghost train business. She was near the station one night, several years ago, and she thought she saw the train.

JULIA. *(Wildly)* I did see it. You know I saw it —I did see it.

STERLING. *(Near JULIA; soothingly)* Now—now, dear.

(LIGHTNING—THUNDER.)

PRICE. *(C.)* You see, she comes from Cornwall, England, and believes in ghosts. She always has, ever since she was a child—I sometimes feel there is something psychic about her. Anyway, she thought she saw this ghost train, and it was a great shock to her. So great a shock that it—well—it upset her permanently. She's perfectly well most of the time, but some nights she has an idea that this ghost train will run, and it has a morbid fascination for her. She feels she must see it again. This is one of her bad nights—now I hope you understand.

JULIA. It will come tonight—I know it will.

PRICE. Nonsense!

JULIA. It's not nonsense. I know it—I feel it! I'm never wrong—that night the tramp died—I felt it, then.

PRICE. *(To the* OTHERS*)* There you are, you see —but don't let it alarm you. How did you get to know this story?

CHARLES. The old Station Master told us the yarn, about an hour ago.

STERLING. Oh, old Saul Hodgkin—where is he, by the way?

RICHARD. Something very strange has happened here tonight.

PRICE. Well?

RICHARD. Old Saul didn't want us to stay here, tonight—he didn't think it was safe.

JULIA. *(Quickly)* There—you see, he felt it, too!

RICHARD. *(Continuing)* He told us the whole story, and said that he was going home.

JULIA. Yes—he wouldn't stay here.

RICHARD. No!

JULIA. I don't blame him. I wouldn't stay here, if I could help it.

PRICE. *(Moving toward* JULIA*)* Good! Then, come along!

JULIA. *(Quickly)* But I can't help it—you know I can't. It's that train. I've got to see it again—I don't want to see it, but I've got to see it. It makes me see it.

PRICE. Never mind about that now. *(Turns to* RICHARD*)* You were saying?

RICHARD. He said he should go home. He took his bicycle-lamp, lit it, and went away. A little while later we heard a noise outside that door, and when we opened it, we found him—dead!

PRICE. Good God!⎫
STERLING. What! ⎭ *(Together)*

JULIA. *(Seated* L.C.*)* I knew it! What did I tell you—now, perhaps you'll believe me.

PEGGY. *(*L., *by stove)* You know it was something supernatural?

JULIA. Yes! That's the way they found poor Ted Holmes—lying outside that door.

STERLING. *(Soothingly)* Steady, dear, steady! *(To the* OTHERS*)* I'm a doctor, ladies and gentlemen. Where is this poor fellow—let me see him.
(LIGHTNING—THUNDER.)

RICHARD. *(*R.C.*)* We carried him into the ticket office.

STERLING. I'll go and examine him. *(Exits up* R., *closing door.)*

CHARLES. *(Crossing a little to up* C.*)* You see the kind of business it is. It gave us a shock.

PRICE. Naturally! *(Crosses to* JULIA L.C.*)* Come along, Julia—it's time to be off.

JULIA. No! No! I must stay—it's that train—everything is bearing me out. That train won't let me go.

RICHARD. There's a lot of difference between the coincidence of two men falling dead and a phantom train.

JULIA. But the death of Ted Holmes was the beginning of it—twenty years ago tonight.

STERLING. *(Enters from up* R.; *leaves door open;*

crosses to RICHARD *down* R.C.*)* Say! What's the joke?

RICHARD. *(*R.C.*)* Eh?

STERLING. It's on us, all right, although under the circumstances, it's not in the best of taste. Where do we laugh?

RICHARD. I don't get you.

STERLING. Didn't you tell us that Saul Hodgkin dropped dead?

RICHARD. Yes—we carried him in there. Why?

STERLING. Go and look.

RICHARD. What the—— *(Exits up* R. CHARLES *crosses after him to up* R.C. *After a slight pause,* RICHARD *returns)* Why, he—he—isn't there. *(Crosses back to down* R.C.*)*

STERLING. No!

CHARLES. *(Up* R.C. PEGGY *and* ELSIE *both rise.)* He must be there. *(Exits up* R. *and after a slight pause, returns)* Good God! *(Crosses across back to* PEGGY *up* L.*)*

PRICE. This joke is beyond me, gentlemen— especially considering my niece's state of health.

PEGGY. But we all saw him.

(LIGHTNING—THUNDER.)

JULIA. *(Suddenly rising)* I've got it! I've got it!

PRICE. What's the matter?

JULIA. *(Crossing to* C. *between* PRICE *and* STERLING*)* Don't you see?

RICHARD. *(Coming a little down* R.*)* See what?

JULIA. It was Ted Holmes.

PRICE. What the devil are you driving at?

JULIA. It's all clear—terribly clear. Listen to me —don't you know that Ted Holmes was a man very similar to Saul Hodgkin? My father knew him well. I'll bet you anything you like that Saul Hodgkin is safe at home in bed, this very minute. It was him you found outside that door—it was Ted Holmes.

(Crosses towards L. and directs the finish of the line to ELSIE.*)*

ELSIE. *(Down L., begins to break a little)* O-o-h!

PEGGY. It couldn't have been—it couldn't!

JULIA. If it was Saul Hodgkin, where is he? A man can't vanish into the air.

RICHARD. This is absurd.

JULIA. *(Crossing to* ELSIE*)* And the time when all this happened—it was eleven o'clock?

CHARLES. Well—yes.

JULIA. *(Turns back to* L.C. *by swivel chair)* I knew it. It *was* Ted Holmes.

PRICE. *(To* STERLING R.C.*)* We've got to get her out of here, somehow. *(Crossing to* JULIA*)* Come along, Julia.

JULIA. Once and for all, I can't come. I am going to stay here. You are trying to drive me mad. You know as well as I do that that train will come. and you pretend it's my delusion. You want to put me away, just as you did before—you are trying to get me put away, but you shan't. I won't stir from here. I'll prove to you that I'm not wrong about this.

PRICE. But I——

JULIA. I won't come—you can kill me if you like, but I won't go. *(Crossing to* C.*)*

PRICE. *(Crosses after her, angrily)* Enough of this!

JULIA. *(Crossing further from him to* C.*)* Don't you touch me. Go 'way—go 'way!

(LIGHTNING—THUNDER.)

STERLING. *(*R.C.*)* Steady, dear, steady! *(Crosses in front of her to* PRICE L.C.*)* Listen to me, Price— why can't you humor her a little? She'll be as right as rain in the morning. Now, why don't you clear off and leave her to me—I can manage her better. You seem to excite her. I'll get her away, I think, and if not, let her stay here. The train won't come, and that may put an end to these attacks of hers. What do you say—is it worth while?

PRICE. Oh, very well! *(Crossing to* JULIA C.*)* I'm going. *(Crosses up; opens door* C.*)* I'm hanged if I'm going to stay around here all night. *(Exits quickly* C.; *closes door.)*

TEDDIE. *(Lying on bench up* R., *rousing a little as* PRICE *exits)* Oh, are you going? Good night!

JULIA. Where is he going?

STERLING. He's going home. Now you have a little rest, and then we'll all go.

JULIA. I'm going to stay here.

STERLING. Very well, dear—just as you like.

JULIA. It isn't what I like—it's because I've got to. It's that train! This place terrifies me—this room is full of eyes—that all stare at me—and stare —and stare—and stare! *(Looks wildly around room)* Oh, why do you look at me like that? You think I'm mad, but I'm not mad—it's this room— it's full of evil.

STERLING. *(Crossing to her)* Then why not come away from it?

JULIA. Why do you keep saying that to me— why are you so cruel? You know I would if I could. Why won't you help me? *(Turns to* RICHARD R.C.*)*

RICHARD. We want to help you.

JULIA. No! No, you don't—you're just the same as all the rest. You're just as afraid of the place as I am, but you won't own it. You blame me.

STERLING. Everything is all right—I'll stay with you.

JULIA. *(Crosses uncertainly to chair* L.C. *and sits)* And, if the thing happens, you won't say I'm mad any more?

STERLING. *(Assisting her into chair)* Of course not! *(To the* OTHERS*)* Everything considered, I think it might be better for you people to follow Price's example, and clear out.

(LIGHTNING—THUNDER.)

RICHARD. I admit it's awkward.

STERLING. *(Turns back to C.)* It's only about five miles to the farm, and only five and a half to Price's house. It might be better to risk the wetting than to bring on any further unpleasant experience.

CHARLES. *(Up L. with PEGGY)* What do you think, Pegs?

PEGGY. Just as you like—I'm not afraid while I'm with you.

ELSIE. *(Down L.)* I think we'd better go. I'm not nervous, of course—but this room is very uncomfortable.

RICHARD. *(Starts to cross down L.)* Very well —we'll go! *(There is a general movement to pick up baggage. ELSIE turns for grip down L. CHARLES and PEGGY turn to up L. for grips.)*

TEDDIE. *(Rises; crosses down R.C.)* What are you all doing?

CHARLES. We're going.

TEDDIE. But, I say, old thing. Just one fleeting moment.

RICHARD. Well?

TEDDIE. *(Indicates MISS BOURNE on table up L.)* How about the Countess?

CHARLES. Good Lord, yes! (ALL *stop movement for baggage.)*

STERLING. *(Seeing MISS BOURNE for the first time, crosses up L.C. to table)* Who's that?

RICHARD. This lady is one of our party.

STERLING. Isn't she well?

RICHARD. Well—hardly!

PEGGY. *(Up L. at end of table)* She couldn't walk five miles even if she were.

Sterling. *(Up* l.c. *by table)* What's wrong with her?

Richard. It's like this, Doctor—it's rather difficult to explain—but she felt very faint, and we persuaded her into taking a little brandy. Something attracted our attention for a moment, and she—she —er——

Teddie. *(Shows empty flask)* She holed out in one. Beats me how she did it.

Sterling. So she's——

Richard. She wasn't used to it.

Teddie. I don't know about that. A capacity like that can't be acquired all in a moment, you know—what?

Charles. *(Up* l. *at table)* You are an idiot.

Teddie. What a head she'll have in the morning.

Richard. *(To* Sterling*)* You see, it puts us in rather a quandary.

Sterling. Leave the lady with us.

Charles. But suppose Miss Bourne should wake —it might give her an awful shock.

Sterling. It's the only way out. *(INCREASE WIND and RAIN.)*

Teddie. *(Crossing to* c.*)* Listen, everybody—I've got a simply topping notion. It's raining outside, and I'm not going to walk five miles in that rotten rain for any ghost. I'll stay here, and help look after Miss Bourne. I think she rather likes me—at least, she ought to, after taking all my brandy!

(INCREASE LIGHTNING and THUNDER.)

Sterling. *(Crossing to* Teddie*)* No! You go with the others.

Richard. *(Down* l. *by* Elsie*)* I think we'd better all stay. What do you think, Elsie?

Elsie. I'm not afraid.

Charles. *(Up* l. *with* Peggy*)* Shall we stick it

out, Pegs? *(DIMINISH LIGHTNING and THUNDER.)*

PEGGY. *(Up* L. *with* CHARLES) I'm game.

RICHARD. *(To* STERLING) That's settled, then—we stay. (ALL *put baggage back in place. DIMINISH RAIN and WIND.)*

STERLING. If you want my opinion, you are very ill-advised.

TEDDIE. Not at all—I think this whole affair is jolly sporting.

STERLING. *(Crosses down* R.C.) Very well—if you've made up your minds. (PEGGY *and* ELSIE *sit again.)*

TEDDIE. By the way—all this reminds me very much of those people who spent the night in the haunted mill. Do you know, they hadn't been there for more than half an hour when they heard——

JULIA. *(Seated* L.C., *leans to him eagerly)* Yes? Yes? What did they hear?

TEDDIE. Well, they heard——

RICHARD. See here—we don't want that story.

TEDDIE. *(Crossing a little to* R.) It's quite a drawing-room story.

STERLING. It would be better to take the ladies away.

JULIA. They say when it comes you hear the bell ringing dismally—frightfully—— I wonder if the bell will ring tonight? Just listen—drip—drip—drop!

STERLING. *(Crossing to her,* L.C., *soothes her)* Steady, dear—steady!

JULIA. *(Rising; to* C.) It's coming, I tell you! It will be here soon! I can feel it! Look—look—— Don't you see—there?

RICHARD. What the——?

STERLING. *(Soothingly)* Julia! Julia!

JULIA. *(Continuing, turning as she speaks and tracing passage from door* R. *to door up* C.) Look!

Don't you see? It's Ted Holmes! He's coming out of the ticket office, with the lamp in his hand—— He's crossing over to the door! He's opening the door! *(Door* C. *opens and closes.)*

RICHARD. *(*L.C.*)* Good God!

STERLING. *(Crosses up to door* C. *and listens)* It's all right—it's only the wind.

TEDDIE. *(*R. *Crossing to door up* R.*)* All this is dashed queer. *(Exits up* R.*)*

STERLING. *(Crossing down to* JULIA C.*)* Come, dear—let's go into the other room. This place isn't good for you. *(Leads her gently to door up* R.*)*

JULIA. *(Turns at door up* R.*; indicates door* C.*)* If you open the door, you will find him there— again. *(Exits, following* STERLING, *up* R. RICH- ARD, *down* L., *starts up* R., *hesitates as if to ask* ELSIE, *then continues across to up* R. *As he is near- ing the door* ELSIE *calls anxiously.)*

ELSIE. Dick! (RICHARD *stops up* R. *She crosses to him)* Shall we go, too?

RICHARD. *(Up* R.C.*)* We may as well. (ELSIE *hesitates as if to take his arm, then draws herself up and exits up* R. RICHARD, *after a glance around the room at the* OTHERS, *exits up* R.*)*

CHARLES. *(Up* L. *with* PEGGY*)* Darling, I'd have given anything in the world to have spared you a night like this. *(Leads her to swivel chair* L.C.*)*

PEGGY. It's not your fault, dear. Perhaps it has its bright side, too. It will teach us to face things together, always.

CHARLES. *(Puts her into chair)* But I can't bear to see you frightened. What can we do?

PEGGY. *(Sitting chair* L.C., *facing front, thinking)* I wonder if that poor girl was right? (CHARLES *lis- tens for sound from outside for a second, then quietly tiptoes up and out door* C. *to* R., *leaving door open, while* PEGGY *continues)* Oh, I must try and control myself—it's silly of me to be frightened

when you're here to look after me. *(Slight pause.)* Charlie, why don't you answer me? *(Slight pause.)* Charlie, where are you? *(Looks around and sees that she is alone. She rises and runs out of the door* C. *to* L., *screaming hysterically)* Oh, Charlie— Charlie! Where are you? Where are you, Charlie? *(Etc.)*

CHARLES. *(Outside, up* C. *to* R., *answering her)* It's all right, Peggy—here I am, dear! *(He comes running back, as* PEGGY *comes rushing into his arms outside the door, screaming and sobbing hysterically. He leads her back inside room, soothing her, closing the door)* It's all right, Pegs. I thought I heard somebody whispering outside, and I went out to see who it was. *(They embrace up* C. *before door.)*

TEDDIE. *(Enters up* R. *very quietly, closes door after him and tiptoes over to them up* R.C.*)* I say! *(They jump apart, startled.)*

CHARLES. *(Sharply)* Yes?

TEDDIE. I want to speak to you two.

CHARLES. Oh—you do?

TEDDIE. Yes! *(Takes* CHARLIE *by the wrist and leads him down stage.* PEGGY *holds onto* CHARLES' *arm and follows.)* I want to warn you about something.

CHARLES. What is it?

TEDDIE. Well—the queer thing is that I don't know. But I feel that it's my duty to warn you.

PEGGY. But what about?

TEDDIE. Well, I've got a sort of a presentiment— a kind of a nasty feeling, you know. I feel that we haven't got over the worst of this yet. *(PEGGY, with a little shudder, crosses and sits, swivel chair* L.C.*)*

CHARLES. There's nothing like being optimistic.

TEDDIE. I know. I'm trying to be—but I feel pretty sure that the worst is yet to come.

CHARLES. Oh, don't talk rot, man.

TEDDIE. But I don't know that it is rot. I want you to promise me something, will you?

CHARLES. It's all according to what it is.

TEDDIE. I want you to promise that if anything unpleasant happens, you will be guided by me.

CHARLES. By you?

TEDDIE. Yes! You needn't look so beastly surprised. I'm not the silly ass that I look.

CHARLES. I didn't think that you could be!

TEDDIE. As a matter of fact, I think I'm rather a cute bird—and I want you to promise to back me up.

CHARLES. What are you going to do?

TEDDIE. That's the funny part about it—I haven't the faintest idea.

CHARLES. *(Sharply)* This is no time for kidding.

TEDDIE. Why, my dear old thing—I was never more serious in my life. *(Taking a small revolver from his pocket and concealing it from audience, in his hand)* Give me your hand.

CHARLES. *(Giving his hand. PEGGY rises L.C. to watch)* Why?

TEDDIE. *(Passing the revolver to him)* I want you to hold this. Don't show it to anyone. Put it in your pocket. (CHARLES *does so.)* Now, do you understand?

CHARLES. No, I don't.

TEDDIE. You don't? Neither do I—but I can depend on you to back me up, can't I?

CHARLES. You're a great fellow to put yourself at the head of a party, aren't you?

TEDDIE. Do you think so, old bean?

CHARLES. No! I'm damned if I do.

TEDDIE. But you will do as I tell you?

CHARLES. *(Crossing to PEGGY)* I shall use my own discretion! *(He crosses with PEGGY to down L.)*

TEDDIE. *(Following to* C.*)* Oh—I shouldn't do that.

RICHARD. *(Entering up* R. *to down* R.C.*, followed by* ELSIE, *who goes a little down* R.*)* I say—you people!

CHARLES. Yes?

RICHARD. I've been thinking this matter over, and I've come to this conclusion. We don't know what we're up against in this place, so we ought to all stand together.

CHARLES. Of course!

RICHARD. I want to know if you're willing to back me up?

CHARLES. *(Standing down* L.*, his hand over* PEGGY'S *shoulder, who is seated beside him in chair down* L.*)* What at?

RICHARD. Well, I don't know—exactly.

TEDDIE. *(Coming down* C.*)* It's a most extraordinary thing that you should say that. I've just been asking them to back me up.

RICHARD. You?

TEDDIE. Yes! Why not?

RICHARD. Hell, I shouldn't have thought you'd be of much use in a crisis.

TEDDIE. Oh, here—I say!

PEGGY. *(Seated down* L.*)* Hush! What was that?

RICHARD. I didn't hear anything.

JULIA. *(Off up* R. *moans)* O-o-h!

ELSIE. It's that poor girl in the other room.

JULIA. *(Entering from up* R. *to down* C.*)* Oh, I can't bear any more of it—I can't!

STERLING. *(Entering after* JULIA *to* R.C. RICH- ARD *crosses up* R.C.*)* It's all right, Julia—it's over now.

JULIA. Over? Why, it hasn't started. Listen, I don't want to frighten you people—but I know what is going to happen, and it's going to happen soon. I can feel it. Listen—there it is again. Drip—drip—·

drip! It will be here soon—just as it all happened before. The scream of the brakes—the shriek of the whistle—louder—louder—louder! So loud that the noise nearly kills me, and I've got to see it again—and if I see it again I may die!

STERLING. Then go away.

JULIA. Why do you keep saying that to me? Why don't you all go away, and leave me?

RICHARD. *(By* ELSIE, R.*)* Because we're not afraid.

JULIA. That makes it all the more dangerous. Oh, why don't you take my advice? You think I'm mad—but I'm not mad. When the train comes——

RICHARD. The train can't come.

STERLING. *(A little up* R.C.*)* We ought to be prepared. I'm not a believer in ghost stories—but I must confess this seems queer business to me.

JULIA. On it came that night, thundering down the valley, and then the brakes jammed on—jarring—tearing!

RICHARD. If the train comes, I'll believe the yarn. Trains can't run around without human beings to control them.

JULIA. The tearing of the brakes, the grinding and the rasping, the shriek of the whistle—and a dead man lying on the platform! And then the roar —louder—louder—and then crash! Into the river below! Oh, don't you hear it? Why don't you go, while there's still time?

RICHARD. We can't go now!

JULIA. Then for God's sake, stop your ears— don't look at it! Remember what has happened to me—be warned—— Oh, be warned!

RICHARD. The train won't come—it's impossible.
(START TRAIN EFFECT and SIGNAL BELL.)

JULIA. The bell! The signal bell! You heard it— Now will you believe me?

STERLING. *(Down* R.C.*)* Damned queer!

CHARLES. *(Down L.)* It might have been the wind that caused that.

JULIA. No—no! The bell—the signal bell! It always rings! *(DISTANT WHISTLE.)*

RICHARD. What's the time?

CHARLES. *(Looking at wrist watch)* One minute to twelve!

TEDDIE. *(R.C. by JULIA)* What was that?

RICHARD. *(R. by ELSIE)* Eh?

ELSIE. *(Down R.)* I think I heard a train whistle!

JULIA. It's coming! It's coming!

RICHARD. Your imagination!

ELSIE. No—no! I'm sure I heard a whistle!

TEDDIE. *(Crossing up to door up C.)* Oh, I'm going to see that!

JULIA. *(Trying to stop him)* No! No! Stop!!! *(DISTANT WHISTLE.)*

RICHARD. By God—she's right!

CHARLES. *(Down L.)* What?

RICHARD. A train! Don't you hear it? *(WHISTLE NEARER.)*

(WARN Curtain.)

JULIA. I knew it!

PEGGY. *(Down L. in CHARLES' arms)* It's coming! It's coming!

CHARLES. *(Down L., protecting PEGGY in his arms)* Steady, old girl!

JULIA. *(C. Continuing)* Thundering down the valley! It's coming! On—on—on!

TEDDIE. *(Running to door up C.)* I'm going to see it! *(He tries door up C.)* It's stuck! (RICHARD *crosses up to him C. and they both try door.)*

(START RUMBLES.)

RICHARD. It's bolted or fastened, somehow! *(Crosses to door up R. and tries it.* TEDDIE *stays at door up C.)* This one is locked too! We're shut in!

CHARLES. *(Rushing across to door up R.)* No!

RICHARD. *(Crossing down to ELSIE down R.)* We

are, I tell you! We're shut in! (CHARLES *is trying door up* R., *then crosses back to* PEGGY *down* L. *and takes her in his arms as the TRAIN roars past the station.* ELSIE *clings to* RICHARD.)

JULIA. *(As the roar of the train approaches, crosses up to window up* L., *then slowly draws back to away down* R.C.*)* Listen to it! Listen to it! I must see it! I must! I've got to see it!

STERLING. *(Down* R.C., *seizing her and trying to restrain her)* Hold her, someone!

JULIA. *(Breaking from him)* Let me go! Let me go! *(She rushes to table up* R. *and jumping onto bench in front of it, seizes the vacuum bottle on the table and crashes it through one pane of the window as the noise of the train is at its climax. As she smashes the glass the glare of the HEAD-LIGHT sweeps through the room, the SMOKE from the engine swirls in, and the RED FLARE of the fire flashes by, followed by the swiftly moving LIGHTS of the coaches. As the train dashes past,* JULIA *on the bench sways, and topples over backward in a dead faint, her fall being broken by* STER-LING, *who eases her to the floor, kneeling beside her as the Curtain is coming down.)*

CURTAIN

FIRST CALL: *Picture.*

SECOND CALL: RICHARD, ELSIE, CHARLES, **PEGGY.**

THIRD CALL: JULIA, PRICE, STERLING.

FOURTH CALL: JULIA.

FIFTH CALL: TEDDIE.

SIXTH CALL AND ALL OTHER CALLS: COMPANY.

ACT THREE

SCENE: *The same as Act II.*

> *The bench which was in front of the table up*
> L. *at the beginning of Act II has been moved to*
> *down, R.C. and the chair from down R. has been*
> *brought out to R.C., with the end of the bench*
> *against it, the two forming a couch.* STERLING'S
> *coat and* TEDDIE'S *air cushion and one of the*
> *cushions brought on by* MISS BOURNE *are on*
> *the seat of the chair to form a pillow, and* TED-
> DIE'S *blue steamer rug has been thrown over the*
> *bench. The swivel chair is in the same position*
> *at L.C. as at the beginning of Act II, and the*
> *straight chair from up L. is now down L. below*
> *stove as in Act II.*

TIME: *Half-hour later. Midnight, the same night.*

AT RISE: *The room is lighted as at the beginning*
> *of Acts I and II. The stove door is now closed,*
> *and the red glow of the fire is gone, the fire*
> *having died out. Both the door up C. and the*
> *ticket-office door up R. are closed, and the ticket-*
> *office window at R. is also closed. The rain has*
> *ceased and there is silence outside. There are*
> *discovered,* JULIA, *lying on the bench R.C., still*
> *in her faint;* STERLING *standing behind the*
> *bench R.C., bending over her;* TEDDIE, *seated on*
> L. *end of bench, R.C., by* JULIA, *looking on;*
> CHARLES *and* PEGGY, *up L. in front of table,*
> *where* MISS BOURNE *still lies asleep; and* RICH-

74

ARD *and* ELSIE, *seated on bench down* L. *As the Curtain rises* STERLING *straightens up and speaks.*

STERLING. *(Straightening up behind bench* R.C.*)* H-h-m-m!

TEDDIE. *(Seated* L. *end of bench* R.C.*)* Flummoxed, eh?

STERLING. Yes, I don't mind owning it.

PEGGY. *(By table up* L. *with* CHARLES*)* You're sure she's not dead?

STERLING. Oh, no, she's not dead! *(Bends again over* JULIA*)* Her heart beat is faint, and yet pretty steady.

TEDDIE. Haven't you got one of those what-do-you-call-em's—those listening-in jiggers?

STERLING. Stethescope, you mean?

TEDDIE. Yes, that's it.

STERLING. No, I've none of my instruments with me—that's the devil of it all.

RICHARD. *(Seated down* L. *with* ELSIE*)* Then you don't know what is the matter with her, Doctor?

STERLING. I don't. She's had these queer turns before, but they've never ended like this. It seems like a stroke of some sort, and yet so many of the symptoms are missing.

TEDDIE. *(Seated* L. *end of bench,* R.C.*)* What symptoms?

STERLING. *(*R.C., *behind bench)* You wouldn't understand if I told you.

TEDDIE. Tell me, and see.

STERLING. You're an extraordinary young man. What do you want to know for? What difference does it make?

TEDDIE. Oh, I don't know, old thing—just idle curiosity. If we're all going to have strokes, it would be rather useful to know when one was coming on, wouldn't it?

ELSIE. *(Seated down L. by* RICHARD*)* You don't think anything else will happen to us?

TEDDIE. Oh, I expect so.

CHARLES. *(Up L. by table with* PEGGY*)* You are a prize idiot.

TEDDIE. I don't know why it is—but you've all got it in for me.

CHARLES. Why can't you shut up? Every time you open your mouth you say something inane.

RICHARD. *(Seated bench down L. with* ELSIE*)* I can't understand it. The train did come, right enough—we can't get away from it.

CHARLES. *(Crossing a little down* C.*)* Then there's Miss—Price—what sent her off like that?

STERLING. I don't know what's the matter with her.

PEGGY. *(Coming a little down* C. *by* CHARLES*)* Don't you remember? She said she saw it—she was just going to tell us about—— Oh, I remember her words—"I saw the driver, and he was——"

STERLING. *(Interrupting)* Of course! That bears out the story of the ghost train—anyone who sees it, dies.

TEDDIE. But, my dear old thing, she's not dead.

STERLING. Not yet!

ELSIE. *(Seated down* L.*)* Then you think——?

STERLING. You can't tell—she's very ill.

ELSIE. *(Turning to* RICHARD, *seated beside her down* L.*)* Oh, it's all so terrible. Dick—Dick! Can't you take me away?

RICHARD. *(Seated down* L. *by* ELSIE*)* My dear girl—the doors are locked, and the windows are barred. We can't get out.

ELSIE. You won't leave me, Dick, will you? I should die if you went away.

RICHARD. *(Soothing her)* I won't leave you, Elsie—don't be afraid.

ELSIE. Oh, I've been a fool, Dick—such a fool.

RICHARD. *(Seated down L. by ELSIE)* Never mind that now, old girl.

ELSIE. *(Seated down L. by RICHARD)* But I do mind, Dick—I mind terribly.

CHARLES. *(Crossing toward R.C. behind bench)* It's a queer thing about this lady—if she hadn't been taken ill she would have told us something about the train.

TEDDIE. *(Seated L. end of bench, R.C.)* She was telling us. It seems as if this train doesn't like being looked at.

PEGGY. *(Sitting swivel chair L.C.)* But how could that make Miss Price ill?

CHARLES. I'm darned if I know.

STERLING. *(Crossing to C.)* Oh, it's no good worrying over this business, ladies and gentlemen. We're up against something too big for us.

PEGGY. Then you really think——?

STERLING. I see no other explanation. When I came here tonight I thought the legend about this place was just a silly local yarn. One must take the facts into consideration, though, and they can't be explained away. If it was old Saul you found outside the door—how did his body get out of the ticket office? There's no window but the skylight. *(Crosses back to behind bench R.C.)*

RICHARD. If only she had told us something more before she fell. *(JULIA, on bench R.C., moves her arm slightly.)*

CHARLES. *(Seeing JULIA's movement)* I say—look!

STERLING. *(R.C., behind R. end of bench R.C.)* What?

CHARLES. She's moving!

STERLING. *(Hastily moving chair from R. end of*

bench to back down R.*)* By Jove—you're right!
(PEGGY *crosses to* R. *end of bench.* RICHARD *rises
to* L.C. ELSIE *rises to* L. *by stove.* TEDDIE *rises and
crosses to down* L. *and sits.* STERLING *comes to front
of bench,* R.C., *and assists* JULIA *to sit up)* Better?

JULIA. *(Says weakly as she sits upright on bench*
R.C.*)* Hello!

RICHARD. Splendid!

ELSIE. She's better?

RICHARD. Yes, I think so.

JULIA. What am I doing here?

STERLING. *(R. end of bench)* It's all right. You
fainted or something. You're better now.

JULIA. How my head aches!

PEGGY. I expect you struck it when you fell.

JULIA. *(Seated on bench* R.C.*)* Fell? Who fell?

CHARLES. *(*R.C., *behind* L. *end of bench)* You
did. Don't you remember?

JULIA. I didn't fall, did I?

STERLING. *(R. by end of bench)* Don't you remember, Julia—you fell off the table.

JULIA. How could I? I wasn't on the table.
(Rises, and sways) Oh, I'm terribly dizzy.

STERLING. *(Quickly crossing to her and support-
ing her)* Sit down, quickly. *(Places her back on
bench.)*

JULIA. What's all this about falling off the table?

STERLING. Surely you remember?

JULIA. I don't seem to remember anything. Yes
—yes, I do. It was the train—I thought it would
come tonight. I have these bad turns sometimes.
They're terrible while they last. I'm sorry—I can
see now how silly I've been. I ought to have known
there was nothing in this stupid ghost business.

RICHARD. What do you mean by "nothing in this
stupid ghost business"?

JULIA. I ought not to have given away, and

frightened you all—— It's all right, the train won't come.

CHARLES. *(Back of L. end of bench R.C.)* But the train did come.

JULIA. *(Seated bench R.C.)* I've been here all the time, haven't I?

CHARLES. Hang it all—you were the only one of us who saw it.

JULIA. Please don't try and frighten me—— What do you mean?

RICHARD. *(L.C., coming a little forward to C.)* He's quite right. Don't you remember, we heard the train in the distance, and then you jumped on the table, to try and get out of the window.

JULIA. That's right, I remember now—I did jump on the table——

RICHARD. And then the train came——

JULIA. No—no—it didn't.

RICHARD. Yes! It came tearing through the station just as you said it would. You broke the window, and after it had gone you turned around and shouted out that you'd seen it.

JULIA. What? The train?

RICHARD. Yes. You said you'd seen the driver, and you were just going to tell us who the driver was when you fell.

JULIA. No—I don't remember—I—no!

STERLING. This is the important point, Julia— who was the driver?

JULIA. The driver?

RICHARD. Yes.

JULIA. I haven't the faintest idea.

RICHARD. But you saw him.

JULIA. I tell you I don't remember anything about it. I—I jumped on the table, and then I must have fainted. I've never fainted before in all my life.

STERLING. *(R. by end of bench)* You fainted, all

right. There's no doubt about that. But it was after the train came, and not before. The question is this: What made you faint?

JULIA. I don't know.

CHARLES. *(Back of* R. *end of bench* R.C.*)* What was it you saw?

JULIA. You know I didn't see anything.

TEDDIE. *(Seated down* L.*, rising to* L.*)* But look here, old thing——

RICHARD. Shut up!

TEDDIE. But I was only going to ask——

RICHARD. Will you shut up? (TEDDIE *turns back and sits down* L.*)* Now look here, Miss Price. You've got to try and pull yourself together and tell us——

JULIA. *(Seated bench* R.C.*)* Stop! Stop! This joke has gone far enough.

RICHARD. Joke?

JULIA. Can't you see I'm not well? I think it's cruel making a fool of me like this. You know I'm nervous and high strung, and yet you do this to me.

RICHARD. No one's trying to fool you—there is no joke.

JULIA. *(Rising unsteadily, and crossing to* L.C. ELSIE *follows.* RICHARD *crosses a little up* L.C.*)* Honestly?

RICHARD. I swear it.

CHARLES. *(Going a little up* R.C.*)* So do I.

JULIA. *(Sways a little)* All I know is that I feel terribly ill. *(Sits in swivel chair* L.C. ELSIE *assists her, then crosses up* L.C.*)*

STERLING. *(Crossing to her to* L.C.*, soothing her)* Now, let's see if we can piece things together a little?

JULIA. *(Seated* L.C.*)* But everything's terribly clear! It wasn't my imagination. We heard the signal bell. Yes. I remember now. We heard the train in the distance—and I jumped on the table—and—and then I fainted!

STERLING. *(Beside her)* Now listen, Julia. This is what really happened: The train came through the station, and you broke the window. *(Pointing to window up L.)* Look—you can see for yourself. After the train had gone you said you saw the driver, and just as you were going to tell us about it, you fell from the table. You gave us a fearful shock. We thought at first that you were dead.

JULIA. I don't remember anything about that. Then the train did come? *(Seated L.C.)*

RICHARD. *(A little up L.C.)* Yes.

JULIA. Yes, but none of you saw it?

CHARLES. *(R.C., back of bench)* Only you. We were locked in here—we couldn't get out.

RICHARD. We can't get out now.

TEDDIE. *(Seated down L.)* Jolly thrilling, isn't it?

JULIA. It's awful! I don't know what we're going to do.

STERLING. We must all get away from here, if we can.

JULIA. I wish to goodness we had! *(The glimmer of a RED LANTERN is seen passing slowly past the windows, outside L. and R., to R., carried by PRICE.)*

ELSIE. *(Up L.C. as she sees lantern passing)* Look! Look! *(ALL stand tensely as lantern passes.)*

CHARLES. *(Going a little up R.C.)* There's someone outside.

TEDDIE. *(Rising to L.C.)* By Jove! So there is. *(Crossing toward door up C.)* Oh—I'm going to see that.

STERLING. *(Turning quickly to up R.C. by door to stop him)* Stop!

TEDDIE. *(Stopping by door up L.C.)* What's up?

STERLING. Have you forgotten the rest of the story?

TEDDIE. I don't quite get you.

STERLING. Who do you think that is out there?

TEDDIE. Someone to open the beastly door, I hope.

JULIA. *(Seated* L.C.*)* Suppose it's Ben Izaacs?

TEDDIE. *(Coming a little down* C. *to her)* Yes, suppose it's Ben—— Say, who is Ben?

JULIA. Haven't you heard the rest of the story? How Ben Izaacs, the driver, went mad?

ELSIE. *(Up* L. *by table)* Yes—yes—they told us that.

CHARLES. It can't be!

STERLING. Who knows?

RICHARD. Don't be a fool, man! *(There is a KNOCK heard at door* C.*)*

PEGGY. *(Down* R.C., *front of bench)* Listen! *(A slight pause.)*

RICHARD. *(Crossing a little toward door)* Who's there? *(Pause)* Come in!

ELSIE. Don't let it.

RICHARD. We must get to the bottom of this. *(There are FIVE more KNOCKS at door up* C.*)*

TEDDIE. *(Crossing down* L.*)* Oh, I'll soon settle that. *(Picking up chair down* L. *and starting for door.)*

JULIA. *(Seated* L.C., *stopping him)* No—no! Don't let it in! Don't!

TEDDIE. *(Putting chair back down)* Oh, all right! I can't do anything around this station.

STERLING. *(Crosses up to door* C. *and listens.* ELSIE *goes up* L. RICHARD *up* L.C. TEDDIE *crosses back down* L. *and sits)* It's gone, whatever it is. *(Turns back down* C.*)*

ELSIE. Thank God for that!

RICHARD. Well, this beats everything!

CHARLES. *(Down* R.*)* You're right there. I wish we knew what the game was.

PEGGY. *(Down* R. *by* CHARLES*)* Charlie—if it had been a man, he would have answered. *(To the*

OTHERS, *coming a step forward to* R.C.) Oh—how many times did he knock?

RICHARD. Six!

PEGGY. Oh!

CHARLES. Well?

PEGGY. I've just remembered something. No—no—I shan't tell you. I might be wrong.

RICHARD. *(Crossing to* C. *to her)* Come along, Mrs. Murdock—we're all in this, you know.

PEGGY. It's—it's too horrible.

CHARLES. Come along, darling—out with it!

PEGGY. Well, it's just this! There were six knocks at the door—the old Station Master said. There were six people killed.

JULIA. *(Seated* L.C.*)* Yes—"Six dead bodies they brought up out of the mud, and they laid them out in this very room."

ELSIE. *(Shudders)* O-o-h!

TEDDIE. *(Seated down* L., *also shuddering)* O-o-o-h-h-h!! (PEGGY *crosses down* R. *to* CHARLES. RICHARD *back up* L. *to* ELSIE.*)*

STERLING. *(Crossing down* L.C. *to soothe* JULIA*)* Julia!

RICHARD. I don't think that's got anything to do with it. We've no proof of it.

STERLING. We've no proof of anything, for that matter.

CHARLES. That's true enough. *(The RED LANTERN carried by* PRICE *again passes windows,* R. *to* L.*)*

ELSIE. *(Up* L., *seeing lantern)* There's that lamp again! (ALL *stand tensely as it passes.*)

SAUL. *(Off* C., *SINGING in a cracked, disguised voice as the lamp passes)* "Rock of Ages, cleft for me——" *(The singing gives way to a wild cracked laugh as the lamp disappears.)*

STERLING. *(Down* C. *by* JULIA*)* It is Ben Izaacs.

JULIA. *(Seated* L.C.*)* What can we do?

ELSIE. I can't stand it, I tell you—I can't!

RICHARD. *(Trying to soothe her)* Steady, Elsie!

ELSIE. I can't stand any more of it—I can't, I tell you.

CHARLES. It's stopped now.

RICHARD. He's gone away.

ELSIE. But suppose he got in—what would we do?

RICHARD. *(Still trying to soothe her)* Come along, Elsie—try and pull yourself together. Whatever it is, it can't hurt us. *(There is a KNOCK at door up* C.*)*

PEGGY. *(Down* R. *with* CHARLES; *gives a moan)* Oh! There it is again.

JULIA. He's trying to get in.

PEGGY. What can we do—what can anyone do?

CHARLES. That's just it—what can we do? Something must be done, or these women will go mad.

RICHARD. *(Up* R.C.*)* God! We'll all go mad, if this goes on much longer.

TEDDIE. *(Seated down* L., *rising to* L.C.*)* I say, you fellows—just listen to me.

RICHARD. *(Coming a little down* R.C., *turning on him)* Shut up! You'll only make things worse.

TEDDIE. But look here!

RICHARD. Shut up, will you!

TEDDIE. There's nothing to get excited about.

RICHARD. Oh, no! What would you suggest?

TEDDIE. Well, I suggest that I sing you all a little song to cheer you up.

RICHARD. *(Angrily)* Shut up!

TEDDIE. *(Singing softly as he crosses back and sits down* L.*)* "Horses, horses, horses——"

STERLING. *(Turning to* JULIA*)* Do you feel well enough to walk, Julia?

JULIA. *(Seated* L.C.*)* Yes, I think so. I'll do anythink if we can only get away.

STERLING. Then you'll go now?

JULIA. *(Rising, L.C.)* Yes.

STERLING. *(Crossing and getting her cloak from bench up* R.*)* Then let's get out of here as soon as possible.

CHARLES. *(Down* R.*)* Where can we go?

STERLING. *(Putting cloak on* JULIA *down* R.C.*)* Anywhere! There should be shelter in a shed or barn somewhere. Anything is better than this, don't you think so?

CHARLES. I do!

RICHARD. *(Crossing to table up* L.*)* But what about this lady?

STERLING. *(Crossing a little up* C. *toward table)* We must rouse her up. At the worst, we can carry her.

RICHARD. Very well. What do you say, Murdock?

CHARLES. *(Crossing to up* L.C.*)* Yes, let's carry her.

TEDDIE. *(Rising to* L.C.*)* But, my dear old thing, you've forgotten something.

RICHARD. Eh?

STERLING. What's that?

TEDDIE. *(Crossing to* R.C. *to bench)* We're fastened in, aren't we? We jolly well can't get out.

STERLING. *(Up* L.C.*)* We can break down the door.

TEDDIE. And then we shall have to pay for the damage. We've broken a beastly window, as it is.

RICHARD. *(Crossing down* C. *to* TEDDIE*)* Well, I'm damned! Who the devil cares about windows?

TEDDIE. *(Sitting bench* R.C.*)* That's right! Go on—be rude—be rude!

RICHARD. Oh, you——! *(Crosses up* C.*)*

TEDDIE. Yes, and there's another thing, too.

STERLING. And what's that?

TEDDIE. *(Rising; crossing a little toward* C.*)* The

ladies were quite right, just now. If we break down the door we shall let that fellow in outside.

ELSIE. *(Up* R.C.*)* Yes! Don't open that door, whatever you do!

PEGGY. *(Up* R.C. *by* ELSIE*)* No—no!

RICHARD. *(*C.*, turning to them)* Now, look here, Elsie—just listen to me, Mrs. Murdock. If it's a man outside, it's quite safe—we're four to one—if it's not a man——

ELSIE. Oh, Dick!

RICHARD. If it's not a man, no locked door will keep it out—do you follow me?

PEGGY. Yes, I suppose you're right.

RICHARD. Look here. Let's have another try. *(He crosses up to door* C. *and tries it.* PEGGY *crosses to* CHARLES, L.*)* This one's still locked. *(Crossing down and starting to pick up bench down* R.C.*)* Let's try and break this one down. *(As he starts to pick up bench* SAUL'S *cracked LAUGH is again heard off* C.*)*

JULIA. *(*L.C. *by chair, hearing the laugh)* Wait! There it is again!

ELSIE. *(Crossing down* R.C. *to* RICHARD*)* We can't go out there! We can't! (CHARLES *and* PEGGY *cross down* L.*)*

(STAGE LIGHTS DOWN SLOWLY.)

STERLING. *(Up* L.C., *near door)* We shall have to face it—it's madness to stay here.

CHARLES. *(As he crosses down* L.*)* Why, something's the matter with the lights.

RICHARD. Good God—they're going out. *(STAGE LIGHTS BLACK OUT.)*

ELSIE. *(Wildly)* No! No! No!

JULIA. *(*L.C. *in the darkness)* There's some devil's work here. Let's go—let's go.

ELSIE. *(Down* R.C.*)* Dick! Dick!

RICHARD. *(Down* R.C. *by her)* I'm here!

JULIA. *(Screaming)* Oh! Something touched

me! Something cold! *(The RED LANTERN car-ried by* PRICE *passes window from* L. *to* C. *only.)*

ELSIE. *(Screaming as she sees lantern)* Look at that! *(DOORS* R. *and* C. *OPEN SILENTLY.)*

TEDDIE. *(Flashing his flashlight through his fingers so that it is only a glow, flashes it to* R. *where* ELSIE *screams, then to* L. *where* PEGGY *and* JULIA *scream, and then on himself up* C.*)* Oh, my God—it's me! *(STAGE LIGHTS ON.)*

JULIA. *(Down* L.C., *seeing doors open)* Look at that.

ELSIE. Why—the doors are open.

JULIA. Yes.

PEGGY. *(Down* L. *with* CHARLES*)* How cold it is!

STERLING. *(Starting up* L.C. *to door)* Come along —let's clear out.

TEDDIE. *(Up* C., *closing door)* Just a moment.

JULIA. *(*L.C. *by chair)* No, we won't wait a moment. We must go quickly—we must.

RICHARD. *(Down* R.*)* Just a second—we must make some arrangements about Miss Bourne.

ELSIE. *(Down* R. *by* RICHARD*)* I shall be afraid to go.

STERLING. We'd better get ready to bolt for it.

RICHARD. I think so, too.

TEDDIE. *(Up* R.C. *near door)* Now, please——

RICHARD. What! Are you starting again?

TEDDIE. I want you all to listen to me, and take my advice.

RICHARD. You're a hell of a fellow to give advice on anything, aren't you?

TEDDIE. In this case, old thing—I am!

CHARLES. Well, what is it?

TEDDIE. I beg that none of us go. Let's all stay here.

STERLING. Stay here? Good Lord, don't listen to the fool. Stay here, indeed.

TEDDIE. Yes—why not?

STERLING. Because we're in great danger. We're up against some devilish thing, and if we stay, God knows what may happen to us. It was different when the doors were fastened—we had no choice in the matten then. Now it's up to us to take the opportunity and quit.

TEDDIE. Yes—but listen, old thing. In spite of it all, none of us has been hurt yet.

STERLING. *(Indicating* JULIA*)* How about this lady?

TEDDIE. She's all right now.

STERLING. Don't talk like a fool. We're not staying a moment longer.

TEDDIE. Right you are, old thing.

STERLING. Then come along.

RICHARD. *(Crossing up* L. *toward table)* Right!

TEDDIE. Bide-a-wee, Prince Charming! (RICHARD *turns up* L.) Leave the "sleeping beauty" alone.

RICHARD. What's the game?

TEDDIE. *(Up* R.C.*)* I'll stay here and look after her. You'll only do the old girl in, digging her out at this hour—especially after the "bun" she was on.

CHARLES. *(Down* L.*)* I don't quite follow you.

TEDDIE. It's quite easy. I'll stay here and look after Miss Bourne—she'll be all right. She won't wake up until morning—that brandy of mine was pre-war.

PEGGY. *(Down* L. *by* CHARLES*)* Aren't you afraid?

TEDDIE. My dear lady, I'm very nearly scared to a pulp.

RICHARD. *(Up* L.*)* Then why——?

TEDDIE. *(Coming a little down* C.*)* Because there's a world of difference between being afraid and running away. Good Lord, what do you think my people would say if they knew I'd been running about the countryside all night, grinning like a dog, and getting my trousers muddy, out of pure funk?

CHARLES. This isn't cowardice—it's common sense. The ladies——

TEDDIE. Oh, I know you're thinking of them.

RICHARD. Now, look here——

TEDDIE. You've been saying, "Now look here," ever since we arrived in this place. I don't want to influence you either way—you all do as you like, and I'll do as I like. All O.K.—what?

STERLING. But we may not have a chance to go later. (RICHARD *crosses* R. *to* ELSIE.)

TEDDIE. (C.) Then run along, my little man.

STERLING. We've simply got to go now.

TEDDIE. I'm not stopping you, am I?

JULIA. (L.C. *by chair*) You're running us all into grave danger—you're trying to drive us mad. You've no right to jeopardize our safety—it's heartless of you.

TEDDIE. Too true, old thing—too true!

JULIA. Then come along, please?

TEDDIE. Now look here! (*To* RICHARD R.) See? I can say "Look here," too! (*To the* OTHERS) Now let's have all this perfectly clear. You can all go and take the ladies with you, and I'll stay here and look after Miss Bourne.

STERLING. (*Angrily*) Enough of this! You're coming.

TEDDIE. On the contrary, my dear sir, I am not.

RICHARD. But why not?

TEDDIE. (R.C., *turning to* RICHARD, R.) Because I happen to be a silly, obstinate ass—and when a silly, obstinate ass like me makes up his silly, obstinate mind, he usually gets his own silly, obstinate way. Now do you follow me?

STERLING. Once and for all, you're not going to stay here alone.

TEDDIE. You surprise me—and what are you going to do about it?

STERLING. Take you by force, if necessary.

TEDDIE. I think not.

CHARLES. *(Down L., coming a little forward)* Steady now, Doctor! I suppose this fellow has a right to please himself, however great a fool he is.

TEDDIE. Thank you, kind sir.

CHARLES. I feel inclined to stay with him.

TEDDIE. Good for you, old bean! Will you stay with me?

JULIA. *(L.C. by chair)* You can't!

CHARLES. *(Turning back L. to PEGGY)* Steady, now. It's like this—I've got my wife to consider.

TEDDIE. Oh, quite!

STERLING. *(Coming up to TEDDIE)* Now listen to me, you young fool!

TEDDIE. *(Up C.)* I listen, you old villain!

STERLING. *(Angrily)* What do you mean?

TEDDIE. Nothing. I'm merely exchanging pleasantries with you. I don't see why you should have a monopoly of all the insults.

STERLING. Why have you made up your mind to stay here?

TEDDIE. Pure cussedness, for one thing.

STERLING. And what else?

TEDDIE. Idle curiosity.

STERLING. What about?

TEDDIE. I want to see what happens next. *(Crossing down and sitting on L. end of bench down R.C.)* I'm going to jolly well sit here, and see that train come back.

JULIA. If we waste any more time it may be too late. *(Runs up C. and throws door open, revealing PRICE in a disguise of engineer's overalls and jumper, with grey wig and beard, and holding the red lantern before him. JULIA starts back to L.C.)* Now perhaps you're satisfied?

TEDDIE. *(Jumping quickly to his feet, drawing a revolver as he does so, and starting for door up C.)*

No! I'm damned if I am! (PRICE *runs off to* R. *as* TEDDIE *starts up for him.*) Now for it! *(He exits quickly* C. *to* R., *following* PRICE, *and there is heard the sound of one SHOT.* TEDDIE *re-enters with the lantern, slamming the door after him, as he shows the lantern)* Look! Blood! Ghost or no ghost, I've winged him. That's that!

STERLING. *(In a panic starting up* C.*)* What have you done?

TEDDIE. *(Up* C.*)* You'll soon see! *(DISTANT TRAIN WHISTLE.)* Listen! The train again!

PEGGY. *(Down* L. *with* CHARLES*)* Oh!! Oh!!

ELSIE. *(Down with* RICHARD R.*)* It's coming back!

TEDDIE. Yes, it's coming back all right, but don't worry. I've got this in hand. I've laid one ghost already, and now I'm going to switch that ghost train onto the siding. *(Turns to go up* C.*)*

STERLING. *(Wildly, crossing to door up* L.C.*)* Stop! Stop!

(APPROACHING TRAIN.)

TEDDIE. *(Turning on him and covering him with gun)* Get back! Up with your hands! (STERLING *backs to up* R.C.*)* Where are you, Murdock?

CHARLES. *(Down* L.*)* Here!

TEDDIE. *(Up* C., *covering* STERLING *with gun)* Remember what I told you? Where's that revolver I gave you?

CHARLES. *(Coming a little forward down* L.*)* I've got it!

TEDDIE. Then watch this devil till I come back! (CHARLES *covers* STERLING *with gun, as* TEDDIE *runs quickly out* C., *slamming door after him. As the ROAR of the TRAIN reaches its climax, there are heard THREE SHOTS. LOUD EXPLO-SION as the train is blown up, together with the CRASH of the train, the HISS of the escaping steam, and the RED FLARE of the explosion. As it dies away.* TEDDIE *re-enters, leaving the door open)* I've done it. I've got it onto the siding.

STERLING. *(Up* R.C. *by door)* Say—what is this?

TEDDIE. *(Up* C.*)* It's no good—the game is up.

RICHARD. *(Down* R.*)* Game? Do you mean this is a trick?

TEDDIE. Yes! These people are at the bottom of it. (JULIA *drops into chair* L.C.*)*

PEGGY. *(Down* L. *with* CHARLES*)* Then there's no ghost train?

TEDDIE. The train is as real as the Montreal Flyer.

(The VOICES of the DETECTIVES *are heard outside* C.*)*

STERLING. I tell you——

TEDDIE. Shut up!

RICHARD. *(Down* R.*)* But what's their object?

TEDDIE. *(Dropping back to up* L.C. *as he hears the voices)* We shall soon know that. *(As* SAUL *and* PRICE, *still with his disguise, followed by* DE-TECTIVES, *enter* C.*)* Here they are. (SAUL *wearing handcuffs,* PRICE *also with handcuffs and a bandage on his wrist.* JACKSON *follows and remains in door, followed by* TWO DETECTIVES, *who remain just outside door.)*

CHARLES. *(Down* L. *as he sees* SAUL *enter)* Why—it's Saul Hodgkin!

TEDDIE. *(Up* L.C. *front of table)* Yes! He's the engineer of that damn train. He got you all with that sham dead trick of his. *(To* JACKSON*)* Got 'em all, Jackson?

JACKSON. I think so.

TEDDIE. *(Pulling off* PRICE'S *wig and beard)* Who's this fellow?

RICHARD. *(As he recognizes* PRICE*)* Mr. Price!

TEDDIE. Yes—he was your Ben Izaacs. *(To* PRICE*)* I thought it was you I winged.

PRICE. You put a bullet right through my arm—damn you!

TEDDIE. Too bad it wasn't right through your head, damn you. Now, then, what's the game?

STERLING. Keep your mouth shut, Price.

PRICE. Oh, I'm no squealer.

PEGGY. Hadn't the doctor better see to his arm?

TEDDIE. Doctor? What doctor?

PEGGY. Doctor Sterling.

TEDDIE. He's no more a doctor than you are. Didn't you see him take Miss Price's pulse with his thumb?

PRICE. *(Angrily to* STERLING*)* You're a fool, Jack.

STERLING. Who the hell is this fellow?

JACKSON. *(Crossing front of* SAUL *to* STERLING*)* Say, haven't you tumbled yet? You ought to know him—Detective Inspector Morrison of Scotland Yard.

CHARLES. A detective!

TEDDIE. Yes! You all had rather a down on me, didn't you?

RICHARD. *(Down* R.*)* Well, I'll be damned!

TEDDIE. Got the train, all right, Jackson?

JACKSON. Sure we got it.

TEDDIE. What was it they were carrying?

JACKSON. Just what we figured! Booze and dope! *(Crosses back up into door* C.*)*

TEDDIE. Dope! Allow me to introduce some rather interesting people. Mr. "Lefty" Jackson of the United States Revenue Office, Washington. *(Indicating* PRICE*)* Mr. Herbert Pineway of London—*(Crossing to* STERLING*)*—and Mr. John Silverton, late of Toronto, head of the Silvernay Mining Company, which is the works a few miles up the line. A nice little collaboration!

RICHARD. Smugglers!

TEDDIE. Right first guess! We've been tracking this gang for two years. That train we've just blown up is loaded with liquor—opium—cocaine—heroin—morphine—and every kind of narcotic. Thanks for your help, Murdock. *(Crossing to* CHARLES *down* L. *and taking gun back.)*

STERLING. You can't pin anything on me!

TEDDIE. Can't I, though? I wasn't sure until to-night—but I made up my mind to get you, especially after you killed Heath.

PRICE. Who's Heath?

JACKSON. That tramp they found dead—one of our best men! *(Pointing to* SAUL*)* Say—you can tell us about that.

SAUL. *(*R. *of door* C.*)* I didn't do it, Mister—I didn't do it. It's their fault, every bit of it.

STERLING. Shut up!

SAUL. *(Facing him)* Oh, it's all right for you—you haven't got no wife and kids dependin' on you. *(Turning to* TEDDIE*)* Fifty dollars a trip they paid me to run that train from the old wharf to the Works—but I didn't know I was haulin' booze and dope. Honest to God, I didn't.

STERLING. That's a lie.

SAUL. It's the God's truth, and you know it. And now I've got to suffer for it. *(With a start for* STERLING*)* Damn you!

TEDDIE. *(Pushing him back)* It's all right, he'll suffer with you. *(Indicating* PRICE*)* Our friend, Pineway here, is wanted by Scotland Yard for murder—that's the reason our department took a hand in the game. *(To* JACKSON*)* Take 'em away.

JACKSON. *(Steps aside from* C. *door as* SAUL *and* PRICE *exit, each escorted by one of the* DETECTIVES*)* Come on, you—outside! *(Taking* STERLING *by the arm)* You too! Lively now! *(Exits* C. *with* STERLING. TEDDIE *closes the door.)*

ELSIE. I don't see it all, even now!

TEDDIE. It's perfectly clear, Mrs. Winthrop. Pineway, who is wanted for murder, is the head of a gang who have been smuggling narcotics into the States for years. He joined forces with Silverton to make a distributing center in this out of the way place for the stuff they smuggled into the country. What put us on to the thing was that Pineway, under another name, was wanted in Europe. The Washington people got a tip and sent Heath to investigate, and he was killed—murdered in this very room.

CHARLES. Then the whole story of the accident was a fake?

TEDDIE. No. An accident did happen, and there's a strong local superstition about the ghost train. Most likely that gave them their idea—anyway it made their job easier, because the natives around here have been taught for years to run for their lives if they heard a train in the night. The great thing was, they didn't want anyone in this room tonight, or the bottom knocked out of the ghost story on which they rely. And so, when the Station-Master found he couldn't get rid of us, he went off to Price's house and told them we were here. Price's house is only half a mile away, not five. There was no time to lose, so they jumped up just as they were in their dinner clothes, and came down here to try and fool us with their bag of tricks. That lamp is no oil lamp, it's wired to the electric current outside. It was all arranged—the faint and all.

RICHARD. But why didn't Saul send us off to Price's?

TEDDIE. Good Lord! They didn't want us there any more than here—this was their busy night.

PEGGY. I'm sure you're wrong about one thing—this poor girl is as innocent as I am. *(Crossing to*

JULIA, *seated* L.C.*)* I understand—I know you're not to blame.

RICHARD. I'm not so sure about that!

TEDDIE. *(Crossing a little to* C.*)* I'm not so sure, either.

(JACKSON *enters* C., *standing in doorway.*)

JULIA. *(Rising)* I—I think I'll be going.

PEGGY. But where will you go?

JULIA. I don't know—this has been too much for me. My head—it's killing me. *(Crossing toward door* C.*)*

TEDDIE. *(Barring her way)* Just a moment!

JULIA. What do you want with me? *(Dropping back to upper* L.C. *by table.)*

TEDDIE. Just who are you?

PEGGY. Why, she's been taken in by this dreadful gang.

JULIA. *(Turning to her)* Yes—yes—you do believe that, don't you?

PEGGY. Poor girl!

CHARLES. *(Down* L. *behind* PEGGY*)* May I see you home?

PEGGY. *(Turning to him, horrified)* Why, Charlie!

TEDDIE. *(To* JACKSON *in door)* Have you got that paper, Jackson?

JACKSON. Not a sign of it, on any of 'em.

TEDDIE. *(Turning to* JULIA*)* Have you got it?

JULIA. What paper?

TEDDIE. We've got an idea there's someone higher up in this, and we've reason to believe that some written message from him is on one of you.

JACKSON. *(Coming a step forward)* And if we get him, there's going to be a lot doing at Headquarters, I can promise you!

JULIA. I don't know what you're talking about.

TEDDIE. *(To* JACKSON*)* We'd better take her with the others if she won't talk.

JACKSON. *(Takes out handcuffs and crossing* L.C. *to* JULIA*)* Oh—I'll make her talk.

JULIA. *(Crossing quickly round to* R.C. *by door)* No! No! For God's sake—not that! I can explain —I do know! (JACKSON *follows a step.)*

TEDDIE. You know where it is? Well, out with it.

JULIA. And there's more I can tell you—a lot more.

JACKSON. *(Coming a step forward)* You bet there is.

TEDDIE. Well?

JULIA. *(Looking about at the* OTHERS*)* But not here—not before all these people—I can't—I can't!

TEDDIE. *(To* JACKSON*)* Are the cars here yet?

JACKSON. They're on their way.

RICHARD. Look here, shall we go and leave you?

TEDDIE. No! *(To* JULIA, *pointing to door up* R.*)* Go in there and I warn you this is a very serious matter for you! (JULIA *crosses toward door up* R. TEDDIE *turns to* JACKSON*)* Leave this to me, will you, Jackson? *(He follows* JULIA *into up* R., *closing door.)*

JACKSON. Right! (JACKSON *goes outside door up* C.; *as he does so, the glare of an auto HEADLIGHT sweeps across his face.)*

ELSIE. I'm perfectly certain that girl knows nothing about it.

JACKSON. *(Stepping back into doorway* C.*)* The motor cars are here, ladies and gentlemen. *(Exits* C. *to* R.*)*

RICHARD. Very well, then let's go! *(Crosses up* R. *and gets coat and hat, then to* C. *and gets bag from under table up* L.C. ELSIE *crosses to up* L., *gets wraps and bag and crosses back to* C. *by* RICHARD*)*

PEGGY. *(Down* L. *to* CHARLES*)* Charlie, dear, do you think they've kept our room at the hotel?

CHARLES. *(His arms about her, reassuring her)* Oh, I'm sure they have. *(He crosses up to L.C. table to get bag. PEGGY crosses down L., getting wraps.)*

RICHARD. *(As CHARLES comes up L.)* Oh, by the way, Murdock, how about a position in my new Boston branch, instead of South America? You're just the man I've been looking for. *(Turning to ELSIE beside him C.)* What do you think, Elsie?

ELSIE. Splendid!

CHARLES. Do you mean that?

RICHARD. I do!

CHARLES. *(Turning to PEGGY, who rushes up to him up L.C.)* Pegs, do you realize what's happened?

PEGGY. *(Embracing CHARLES)* Yes, dear!

RICHARD. *(Handing CHARLES a card)* Look here. Here's my card. Look us up when you get back—say in about ten days' time. And think of us when you're on your honeymoon—we're just starting on our second. *(Turning to ELSIE, beside him)* Isn't that so, Elsie?

ELSIE. *(Embracing him)* Yes, darling! *(They kiss and exit C. to L.)*

CHARLES. *(Embracing PEGGY)* Dearest, isn't that wonderful?

PEGGY. Darling, now you won't have to go away.

(Together.)

TEDDIE. *(His VOICE heard off up R.)* I don't believe a word you're telling me. You're wasting my time. I—— *(JULIA enters up R., TEDDIE following close after her as he speaks.)*

JULIA. *(Suddenly turns just inside door up R., throws a handful of snuff in TEDDIE'S eyes, gives him a sudden push backwards through the door, and slams it, shooting the bolt. CHARLES starts forward to C., front of door. JULIA whirls on him and covers him with a revolver)* Stick 'em up!

PEGGY. *(Panic-stricken)* Oh, Charlie!

CHARLES. *(Putting up his hands)* What does this mean?

JULIA. *(Coming forward to upper* R.C.*)* It means, little man, that I hold all the cards. Well, well—to think that little fool should try to pull the wool over my eyes!

PEGGY. *(Back of* CHARLES*)* Who are you?

JULIA. Oh, don't you worry about me. I'm finger-printed at Scotland Yard, all right. *(Threatening* CHARLES *with gun)* Now, get out of my way. Get out of my way.

CHARLES. *(Up* C. *at door)* I'll be damned if I do.

JULIA. You'll jolly well be if you don't. This is where I kiss you goodbye, and you're going to stand away from that door.

CHARLES. No!!

JULIA. Yes! I'm not fooling! When I shoot, I don't miss, and your little sweetie there will be a widow. Come on now, make up your mind, quick! One—two——

PEGGY. *(Seizing* CHARLES' *arm, pulls him back to her up* L.C.*)* Oh! For my sake, Charlie!

JULIA. *(Crossing to door* C. *and backing out through it, still covering* CHARLES *and* PEGGY *with the gun)* That's right! She's got more brains than you have. I'm the devil's grandmother—— (TEDDIE *suddenly enters* C. *from* R., *followed by* JACKSON, *seizing* JULIA'S *arms and pinning them behind her.)* Oh, blazes!

TEDDIE. *(To* JACKSON, *who is helping him hold her arms)* Would you mind putting the bracelets on "the devil's grandmother," old bean? (JACKSON *handcuffs* JULIA; *remains in the doorway, as* TEDDIE *takes a step forward into the room.)*

JULIA. *(Taking a step forward beside* TEDDIE*)* Say! Are you one or two?

TEDDIE. I'm one too many for you, what?

JULIA. How did you get out of there?

TEDDIE. You forget that our mutual friend, Saul, has a secret way out of that room. I found it.

JULIA. *(Nudging him with her shoulder)* My Gawd! Say, you and I ought to do business together. *(She is moving her jaws as if chewing.)*

TEDDIE. What are you chewing?

JULIA. Not gum! That's that little bit of paper you're after. *(She swallows the contents of her mouth with a choking cough)* Now, go after it—and you'll have a long ways to dive for it! *(She swallows and coughs again)* All gone!

JACKSON. *(In door C.)* You'll get yours, all right!

(WARN Curtain.)

JULIA. *(Over her shoulder to him)* Oh, don't you worry—I'm not yellow, and I'll take what's coming to me with a laugh. Well—are we ready?

JACKSON. *(Harshly, drawing back a step)* Yes!!

JULIA. All right, then, let's go! Nightie-night, everybody! *(With a laugh, she exits C. to R., followed by JACKSON.)*

TEDDIE. Just a nice little snow-bird!

PEGGY. *(Up L.C., turning to CHARLES L., behind her)* And you wanted to see her home!

TEDDIE. *(Crossing to up L.C. by end of table, and indicating MISS BOURNE, who is lying on it)* We've only got one little trouble left—here it is.

CHARLES. *(Seeing MISS BOURNE stir slightly, comes up L. with PEGGY by L. end of table)* She's moving! *(Bending over her)* Miss Bourne! Miss Bourne!!

MISS BOURNE. *(Shakily sitting up on table)* Oh! I've got such a headache.

TEDDIE. Cheer up—the cars are here. We'll soon be safe in Rockland.

MISS BOURNE. I'm so glad nothing exciting happened.

PEGGY, CHARLES *and* TEDDIE. *(Together)* Good Heavens!!

CURTAIN

CALLS

FIRST CALL: *Picture*.

SECOND CALL: COMPANY.

ALL OTHER CALLS: COMPANY.

"THE GHOST TRAIN"

PROPERTY PLOT

ACT I

Train effect. (As described.)
Time-tables.
Chalk.
Railroad tickets.
2 calendars.
Lithograph.
Railway maps.
Old trunk, roped.
Coal hod, shovel, poker.
Lantern (Saul).
Telegraph instrument.
Trunks, milk cans, etc.
Bag (Richard.).
Bag (Elsie).
2 Bags (Charles).
Bag (Peggy).
Parrot cage (Miss Bourne).
Cushions, rugs (Miss Bourne).
Golf bag (Teddie).
Kit bag (Teddie).
Rug (Teddie).
Newspaper (Teddie).
Air cushion (Teddie).
Vacuum bottle (Teddie).
Money (Charles).
Rice and confetti (Charles).
Bicycle lamp (Saul).
Matches (Saul).

ACT II

Cigarettes and matches (Elsie).
Flask (Teddie).
Small revolver (Teddie).

ACT III

Red lantern (Price).
Flashlight (Teddie).
Revolver (Teddie).
Handcuffs (on Price and Saul).
Grey wig and beard (Price).
Bandage (Price).
Handcuffs (Jackson).
Revolver (Julia).

TRAIN EFFECTS

1 engine bell.
1 garden roller propelled over bevel-edged struts screwed to stage, 30 inches apart.
1 18-gallon galvanized iron tank.
1 thunder sheet.
Air cylinders.
1 bass drum and pair of sticks.
2 side-drums.
1 small padded mallet (auctioneer's hammer).
1 large padded mallet (for beating tank).
1 medium mallet.
1 wire drum brush.
1 milk churn.
1 pea-whistle.
1 train whistle (for mouth).
1 whistle on cylinder.
2 electric or hand-driven motors.

2 slides cut to give shadows of carriage windows of train.

2 flood arcs on each side of stage.

1 tin amplifier for steam with a counterweight placed in its mouth.

To Work First Train

Screw whistle into nozzle of cylinder.

1 man sits astride this and another cylinder with amplifier ready to work (A).

1 man stands by roller (B).

1 man stands by tank with large padded mallet (C).

1 man stands by thunder-sheet (D).

2 men stand by motors (E).

2 men stand by flood arcs with slides focussed on exterior of windows (F).

1 man stands by with wire brush and small side drum (G).

1 man stands by bass drum (H).

On the rise of the curtain, Signal Bell. C and H beat on tank and drum gently, gradually increasing in volume. Then E and G start, followed by D. Finally A starts air release, and as the total volume of sounds increase, B starts to pull his roller over the struts as rapidly as possible, gradually slowing. When noise is at its height, all *stop dead* except A, who continues to blow off air. While train is in station, Stationmaster shouts, "All change!" "All change!" while C repeatedly beats milk churn with its lid. He stops as Stage Manager blows pea-whistle. A gives two sharp blasts on his whistle (H has carried his bass drum to R. side of stage while train is in station). Stage Manager then grasps medium padded mallet and beats second side drum (which should be fairly slack) 1 beat. Then another beat, then another, gradually increasing in pace and diminishing in volume as train is supposed to leave station. *Simultaneously, and keeping in time with him,* D gives a shake to sheet, A gives puff of steam, B gives beat on tank, E works motors and B starts roller. H also does roll on drum. These effects should be carried on until noise of train dies away in the distance in an indistinct murmur. As train leaves station F slide their slides across the window in turn, gradually increasing in pace to give the effect of the train lights passing the waiting-rooms. *The whole success of the Effect depends on each unit being together and the rhythm preserved.*

To Work Second Train

In this train it is necessary to have three cue lights worked from switchboard fixed so that all the effects men can see them. When the Stage Manager blows whistle for train in distance C and H start as in the first train, E then starts with G, then D joins in. When Peggy says "It's coming! It's coming!" Stage Manager should switch on his first cue light. This should bring A with steam, and other effects, except B, to nearly forte. When Julia turns to run up to window, he switches on second cue light. This should bring in *all* effects double forte, including B and A's whistle. When Julia throws bottle through window, red flare followed by flash-box, at L.C. window, fractional pause, then red flare and flash box through R.C. window. At end of first picture switch on third cue light. On this, all effects must *stop dead.*

To Work Third Train

Only A, B, E, G and H are required for this train. B works his roller over the bare stage in this effect and *NOT* over the struts.

When Teddie says, "You'll soon see," the Stage Manager blows his train whistle (mouth), H starts

gently on drum, giving beat of a train puffing up hill.
A and G keep time with him. The sound gradually
increases until Teddie exits. When it comes up to
forte but still maintains its steady beat B joins in.
Explosion. Silence.

THE LOST CHRISTMAS

Christmas play. 1 act. By Bruce Kimes.

4 males, 3 females. Interior. Modern costumes.
35 minutes.

This charming and sentimental comedy tells of the final and ultimate defeat of Miss Harriet Russell in her personal campaign against Christmas. In a warm and tender scene filled with mingled laughter and tears, Miss Harriet, at long last, comes to know the true meaning of The Lost Christmas.
(Royalty, $5.00.) Price, 60 cents.

THE CHRISTMAS ANGEL

Comedy. 1 act. By Peg Lynch.

7 males, 2 females. Interior. Modern costumes.

Ethel finds that Albert threw a snowball accidentally, breaking the parsonage window, and then ran away. Naturally, when the Rev. Sheridan comes to call they assume he has arrived for retribution and Albert's conscience traps him into agreeing to be an angel in the Christmas pageant.
(Royalty, $10.00.) Price, 60 cents.

CHRISTMAS, INCORPORATED

Christmas play. 1 act. By Walter Kerr.

7 females. Interior. Modern costumes. 35 minutes.

Mary Daly, who works in Conners Dept. Store, decides to quit because Christmas is being savagely destroyed by gross commercialization. A child asks her where she is going. Mary questions the child about Christmas. The child easily explains away the contradiction of sixty seedy Santa Clauses and reveals a feeling for the season very close to Mary's own memory of it.
(Royalty, $5.00.) Price, 60 cents.

DOUBLE DOOR

Drama. 3 acts. By Elizabeth McFadden. 7 males, 5 females. Interior. Costumes, 1910.

An outstanding success on Broadway. Its theme is the battle for power that goes on in an old New York family and culminates on the verge of murder. "This one reserves especial thanks and hearty praises. It returns us to expertness and fascination and fine mood in the theater."—Gilbert Gabriel in *New York American*. "At last a play has come to town that can be heartily recommended. Sturdy theater, compelling. Once you are within the radius of *Double Door* you will remain transfixed until you know what's behind it."—Bernard Sobel, *Daily Mirror*. "*Double Door* is a thriller of a new kind, beautifully written, superbly played, clean as a whistle, and arousing in its spectators a tenseness of interest I have rarely seen equaled in ـ playhouse."—E. Jordan, *America*. Leading part acted by Mary Morris in America and by Sybil Thorndike in London. A play that will challenge the best acting talent of Little Theatres and colleges.

(Royalty, $25.00.)

PRIDE AND PREJUDICE

Comedy. 3 acts. By Helen Jerome. 10 males, 16 females. 3 interiors. Costumes, 1796.

An immensely successful production in New York and London. The play concentrates on Mrs. Bennet's determination to get her daughter married. Jane, Elizabeth and Lydia are likely-looking girls in an unlikely-looking period when a woman's one possible career is matrimony. To be a wife was success. Anything else was failure. Jane and her Mr. Bingley, and Lydia with her Mr. Wickham, are quite content with the god of things as they are, but not Elizabeth! She actually refuses to marry Mr. Collin, whom she openly deplores, and Mr. Darcy, whom she secretly adores. The play is the story of the duel between Elizabeth and her pride and Darcy and his prejudice. Each gives in before the evening is over and pride and prejudice meet halfway. An ideal costume play for schools, colleges and Little Theatres. "This particular reviewer went to the Music Box last night prepared to be bored, and remained to be interested.'—Percy Hammond, *N. Y. Herald Tribune*. "An intelligent script."—Brooks Atkinson, *N. Y. Times*. In ordering please mention name of author of this version.

(Royalty, $25.00.)